GRAFFITI D'ITALIA

BY

W. W. STORY

WILLIAM BLACKWOOD AND SONS
EDINBURGH AND LONDON
MDCCCLXVIII

PREFACE.

THERE are two statements to be made in regard to this volume. First: many of the poems have been previously published in various magazines, though they are now for the first time collected. Second: all the poems are intended to be dramatic in their character; and, being the utterances of historical or purely fictitious personages, are not to be understood as expressing the opinions or sentiments of the Author.

CONTENTS.

MEDIEVAL.

ANTIQUE.

MODERN.

SCHERZI.

AL MIO AMICO

ARTURO DEXTER

Belli gli estivi giorni a me sì cari
Sotto d' Italia il ciel splendido e puro,
Belle le sere avvolte in velo scuro
Che teco io scorsi in dolci favellari;
Più belli ancor, più dolci e più felici,
Perchè su suol stranier vivemmo amici.

Sotto all' ombra di pampane contorte
Ricorda ch' io scrivea la storia mesta
Di due ch' amor sospinse a fin funesta,
A morte l' un, l' altro a peggio che morte!
Or questa istoria a Te consacro, un pegno
Dell' amicizia mia, sebbene indegno.

ROMA, 11 *Aprile* 1866.

MEDIEVAL

GINEVRA DA SIENA.

"Meglio é morir che trarre
Selvaggia vita in solitudin, dove
A niun sei caro e di nessun ti cale."
Saul di Alfieri, scena 4, atto I.

"Love is a greater lawe (by my pan)
Than may be yeven of any erthly man;
And therfore positif lawe, and swiche decree
Is broken all day for love in eche degree.
A man moste nedes love maugre his head.
He may not fleen it, though he shuld be ded,
All be she maid or widewe or elles wif."
CHAUCER: *The Knight's Tale.*

So then you've come at last, my own best friend,
My youth's friend—never friends like those of youth!
I had not thought to see your face again,
Nor any human face that pitied me.
Now let me weep upon your breast; my heart,
Dried up within me, seems to swell again
At your soft touch of pity—let me weep!
My tears so long have burnt me, but these tears,
Like rain on withered grass, bring up again

The old spring greenness. Oh! at last, at last,
This passionate tension of my life gives way.
The desolating sand-spout whirled along
My desert life, and straining up for years
All feelings, thoughts, and hopes, breaks down at last;
So, let me weep here—at your very feet;
Lift me not up—it soothes and calms me so.
See! what a poor, bruised, broken thing am I!
But you, dear Nina, knew me ere this brow
Was ruled with wrinkles, ere the thick dark hair
Which clustered round it grew so thin and white;
One curl at least remains of what it was,
And still you wear it in your locket, love.
You yet are fair. Stop! let me look at you;
How young you are, and I, so old, so old!
'Tis only happiness can keep us young.
Then, how should I be young,—imprisoned here
In this drear villa, all my turbulent thoughts
Storming against my fate, my hopes burnt out,
My heart the crater where their scoriæ lie.
Yet all keeps young about me—all's the same
As I beheld it when a little girl.

These walls are still the same; the sky's the same;
The same sad stretches, the same undimmed stars;
The olives are not changed; there stand the pines,
Murmuring and sighing still; clouds come and go,
Just as they did when I was young and gay:
And looking on them thus, year after year,
So changeless, while 'tis all so changed with me,
Half maddens me at times. They seem to mock
With their perennial youth my vanished joys.
Here, in this room, I was so happy once!
Here, in this room, I am so wretched now!
My ghost—a pleasant, laughing, careless ghost—
Walks down along that terrace. See! 'tis there!
And yours is with it. Ah! one sees that's yours;
But mine—who'd ever dream that once was I?

Look now, it beckons, laughs, and flings a flower.
Off! off! I hate you; vanish from my sight:
There—down the cypresses go—go, I say;
Vanish! and never let me see you more.

'Tis gone now—gone—would it were never there!

Mere fancy, Rosa says—perhaps she's right—
Such tricks things play us. Do not look so strange;
Who can avoid all meetings with one's ghost?
And yours, does yours come never from the past,
From corners dim of olden days and dreams,
To whisper words that almost drive you mad?
Ah! I forget! You are so happy still,
And joy's gay laughter chases ghosts away.

Well, we'll not talk of that, nor think of that,
Only don't look so sad and shake your head;
You know I do not think 'twas really there,
But then it somehow seemed as if it were
Just for a moment's space. Pray bear with me,
And if my ways and words to you seem strange,
Don't mind them, dearest; living all alone
We get fantastic notions, and one's talk
Grows wild with too long talking to one's self.
But now you come and love me, I am strong;
You, with your happy smile, scared from my breast.
Well, well—no matter what,—'tis fled away;
You see it's gone now—look, there's nothing here.

Let them all go; one leap to other days.
My heart is almost light to see your face.
Oh! kiss me, dearest, kiss me yet once more—
How it smooths out the tangles in my brain—
And put your hand in mine: believe me, dear,
For years I have not felt so sane and calm.

I'll write upon your heart as on a book.
If I go over all the old, old days,
You'll listen, will you not? I know you will.

Let me go back to when I saw you last.
Our lives till then had close together lain,
Shaped each to each in habit, feeling, thought,
Like almonds twinned within a single shell.
What thought or hope was mine that was not yours?
What joy was mine that was not shared with you?
All was so innocent when we were girls;
Our little walks—the days you spent with me
In the old villa—where, with arms loose clasped
Around each other's waist we roamed along
Among the giant orange-pots that stood

At every angle of our garden-plot,
And told our secrets—while the fountain plashed,
And, waving in the breeze, its veil of mist
Swept o'er our faces. Think of those long hours
We in the arched and open loggia sat
Pricking the bright flowers on our broidery frames,
And as we chatted, lifting oft our eyes,
We gazed at Amiata's purple height,
Trembling behind its opal veil of air;
Or on the nearer slopes through the green lanes,
Fenced either side with rich and running vines,
Watched the white oxen trail their basket-carts,
Or contadine with wide-flapping hats
Singing amid the olives, whose old trunks
Stood knee-deep in the golden fields of grain.
Do you remember the red poppies, too,
That glowed amid the tender green of spring—
The purple larkspur that assumed their place
Mid the sheared stubble of the autumn fields—
The ilex walk—the acacia's fingered twigs—
The rose-hued oleanders peeping o'er
The terraced wall—the slanting wall that propped

Our garden, from whose clefts the caper plants
Spirted their leaves and burst in plumy flowers?
All these are still the same—they do not miss
The eye that loved them so; and yet how oft
I wonder if those old magnolia-trees
Still feed the air with their great creamy flowers,
And show the wind their rusted under-leaf.
I wonder if that trumpet flower is dead.
Oh heaven! they all should be, I loved them so;
Some one has killed them, if they have not died.

But you can see the villa any day,
And I am wearying you. Yet all these things
Are beads upon the rosary of youth,
And just to say their names recalls those hours
So full of joy—each bead is like a prayer.
How many an hour I've sat and dreamed of them,
And dear Siena, with its Campo tower
That seems to fall against the trooping clouds,
And the great Duomo with its pavement rich,
Till sick at heart I felt that I must die.
People are kneeling there upon it now,

But I shall never kneel there any more;
And bells ring out on happy festivals,
And all the pious people flock to mass,
But I shall never go there any more.
How all these little things come back to me
That I shall never see—no, never more!
Oh, kiss the pavement, dear, when you go back!
Whisper a prayer for me where once I knelt,
And tell the dead stones how I love them still.

These little things,—ah, suffer, love, like me!
You'll know how all these memories live and sting;
Even lifeless things, that scarce with conscious sense
We gaze upon in sorrow or in joy,
Cling to our joy and sorrow close as life.
Things, too, at discord with our lifted mood
Their trivial figure on the mind will stamp
So deep that time can never wipe it out;
Yes, even the pattern of the pavement there,
Its stones a step apart on which I trod
In torturing hours, are printed on my heart

Like some essential part of all I felt;
And when the pang comes back, they, too, return.

As we two wandered, little ignorant girls,
With childish talk and childish wonder then,
What did we know of life?—'twas all a play—
A picture—some few pretty shifting scenes
Set in the magic lantern of our youth.
What could we know, we little hermits, then?—
Watched over, tended, gently led along
A path with ne'er a stone to trip us up;
Reading such innocent books, going to mass,
Saying our Aves every morn and eve;
Never let go beyond a vigilant eye
To watch where danger hovered; caged like birds
In our home aviary, where we sang,
And fluttered round, but never could get out;
Where, though the eagle and the swooping hawk
Were ranging round, we were so safe from them.
How were we fit, thus nurtured, to be loosed
Upon the world? One might as well set free
The frail canary, bred within a cage.

Oh! in the storm and buffet of my life
My heart has flown so often back again,
And beat the bars that could not let me in.

Look at the foolish way in which we're trained,
And say, how can it fit us for the world?
The doctrine and the mass, of course, we're taught;
Then comes our first communion in the fold
Of some clean convent, 'mid the patient nuns,
Whose minds and lives are stunted at the best.
What can they teach beside hypocrisy,
To check the natural currents of our youth?
Through their religious panes they show the world
All glare and falseness—yet we sigh for it;
Then, taken back, we're kept beneath a glass,
Like some frail plant that cannot bear the breeze.
For home is but a kind of convent, where
Our mother is the abbess—we the nuns;
We learn our letters, but there's nought to read
Save tedious homilies and bloodless books.
Life is more real, so we sigh for it—
Not life on this side marriage, but beyond.

For what is life so-called to us poor girls—
Embroidery and trivial talk at home,
Dressing, a little music on the lute, and then
A dull and formal walk on the parade,
Where we may learn to smile and bow with ease.
Sometimes convoyed into society,
Our mother leads us with a careful string,
And lets us hop a little way alone;
But watching us the while with Argus eyes,
And lecturing our manners and our words.
Peeps at the world, from under down-dropped lids
Of fear and innocence, we catch; we're told
That this we must not do—nor that—nor that;
All that we long for is prohibited.
Burn though we may for liberty and joy,
In whose fresh air the heart alone expands,
With little worldly maxims we are drilled;
Calm and reserve alone are maidenly.
We must not speak unless our mother nods.
So life, with all its stern realities
To us is vague, as is a blind man's thought
Of colours, or a deaf man's dream of sounds.

Some day our mother calls us to her room,
Count This, Marchese That, has asked our hand—
She says, "'Tis all arranged for you, my dear;
He's rich and young, and of such noble birth,
We could not ask or hope a better match;
I and your father both are satisfied."
"But I," you cry, "'tis I must marry him;
And I am yet so young, so happy here.
Besides, I've scarcely seen him, know him not—
How can I marry if I do not love?"
"Love—love, of course; first marry, and then love!"

Thus marriage opens unto us the door
That leads to liberty, if not to love.
When we are married, we at least are free;
So, unprepared in ignorant innocence,
We rush to marriage just for freedom's sake.

What could I hope? My little bark put forth
Into the stormy world, and made a wreck,
And here I rot—all dashed to pieces here!

Look at that ghastly hulk there on the beach—

That broken, bare-ribbed skeleton that lies
Deep sunken in the barred and shelving sand;
'Twas a gay vessel launched in pride and joy,
With streaming banners and with music, once—
Look at it now! Then turn, and look at me!
Are we not both the same sad broken wrecks?
Still old thoughts cling, the shells and barnacles
Of happy days, when through the southern seas
Of youth my keel went rushing joyously,
And all my pennons flew, and my white sails
Rounded their bosom to the swelling air.

You know the Count, the husband that they gave—
Cold, stern, impassive, like an angled wall—
Squared to his duties—rigorous, even, hard—
I beat myself to death against that wall.
He married me as he would buy a horse,
Then all was over. "Put it in the stall,
Caparison it well for gala days,
Break it to worldly paces with a curb,
And give it best of food and best of straw."
Kind treatment this, you say: what would you more?

Nothing, unless one has a heart and brain;
And I, alas! was born with one at least.

Ask of the world his character—they'll say,
An honourable man formed to respect,
Proud of his birth; but who would not be proud?
Refined, exact, punctilious; one, in fact,
Safely to trust in great and little things.

Well, then, I trusted him with all I had.
Now, ask of me what was the noble Count?
The world's half right; but half right's wholly wrong.

Fair was his outward seeming—manners fair—
A little stiff with over-courtesy,
Like to those rich brocades all sewn in gold;
But noble, I agree, and dignified.
The apricot is smooth upon the skin,
And yet it only has a stone for heart.
What education teaches, he had learned;
But on a rock you cannot rear a rose.
Still, stoniest natures have their sunward side;
And there with him his pride and honour grew.

The shortest line's the straightest 'twixt two points,
And the frank nature takes it openly.
His nature was secretive : on his path,
Lead where it would, he loved no human eye ;
Dark windings, devious ways, he rather chose.
Fifty miles round, beyond the sight of man,
Rather than one across in open view.
His good and bad alike he loved to hide ;
Spoke little, hated praise—suspected it—
And yet was flattered by obedient acts.
Passions he had, but he had mastered them,
And loved and hated in a bloodless way ;
But never was with generous anger fired,
Nor blazed to indignation at a wrong.
His impulses he doubted—would not stir
To passion's trumpet ; but lay long in wait,
Ambushed—then struck with slow and proud resolve,
And called it justice when he took revenge.

His dark impassive face was cold as bronze ;
His mouth locked up in silence like a chest
Whose key is lost, or drawn as it had worn

A life-long curb ; his forehead full and bare,
Where not a wrinkle told what passed within.
Sometimes his hands would twitch when he was moved,
But not his lips—no, nor his cold round eyes,
From which he shut all meaning at his will ;
While, like an intricate machine, his mind
With counter-wheels worked out the simplest act.

There is my master ! there's the inside man !
Why further then dissect? He, proud and cold,
Reserved, and hating every show of heart ;
I, warm, impetuous, urged by impulses—
Demanding love in words and tones and acts.
Could we two live together? Yes ; as lives
The passionate wave with the affronting cliff,
Fretting in quiet seasons, madly dashed
With useless violence when roused in storm.
How many a time, in longings vast and vain,
I rushed towards him—strove to overclimb
His walled-up nature, and, forced back again,
Fell with a wild lament into myself,
Shattered with struggle, in a dull despair.

When in fierce mood I once o'erstept the line
Of rigid prudence, strict punctilio,
And in strong language railed against the world,
With all its busy, peeping, prying eyes,
He turned with half a smile and half a frown,
And used a figure—'twas the first and last
He ever used save one :—" You like these tropes—
Here's one : your sail is larger than your craft ;
Take heed the first gale do not sweep you down."

" Better go down," I cried, " on the broad sea,
Battling a noble voyage with wind and wave,
Than rot inactive, anchored in the port,
Fixed stem and stern—a hopeless, helpless, hulk.
What if I vail my spirit-sails in fear
And creep to shelter for ignoble rest ?—
The dullest wreck will at its cable strain
When from the outer sea the great swell rolls,
And no poor creature with a heart and brain
But in the stagnant harbour of routine
Feels stormy lifts of longing—pants for life,
And strains to grapple with some noble task."

He smiled half-sneering, and then coldly said,
"The noblest task is to command one's self;"
And then I knéw how huge a fool I was,
And locked my life and longings in my heart.

But after all 'tis love that most we need;
Love only satisfies our woman's heart,
And even our ambition looks to love;
That given, life is light—denied, is death.
Man is content to know that he is loved,
And tires the constant phrase "I love" to hear;
But woman doubts the instrument is broke
Unless she daily hear the sweet refrain.

Thus life went on for three long weary years.
I should have fallen broken to the earth
The last sad year, but one hope buoyed me up—
I was to be a mother. Ah! the thought
Of that dear face, long, long before it came,
Shone in my thoughts with strange pathetic light,
Like the moon shining in a snake-filled dell—
Something at last to have which I could love!

Oh! how I prayed that it might be a boy,
And mediate 'twixt that iron heart and mine.
Who knew? The sternest natures are not whole;
Some vulnerable point there is in all,
Where they were held when dipped into the Styx—
Some mother's touch where you can reach the quick.
So with this reed I helped my hope along,
And, waiting patient, said, "If 'tis a boy
'Twill touch his pride—his pride may touch his love."

Our boy was born, and my prophetic heart,
Like other prophets, mixed the true and false;
His pride was touched—his love was still unborn.
In his first joy there seemed a kind of mist
About his heart—it passed like breath on steel;
At sudden times, as if against his will,
Words almost tender from his lips there came,
Then chased away as weak and out of place;
So with an iron glove one wipes a tear
Quickly, as not belonging to a man.

Sometimes I held him up unto the Count,

And, smothering him with kisses, cried aloud,
"Is he not lovely? oh, my life in life!
My little angel out of paradise!
Say, is he not too dear to stay with us?"
Then he—"Why always thus exaggerate?
An angel? no, a good stout healthy boy;
And dear, of course, because he is our child."
Yet this I thought was half in awkwardness
(Men are so, often, even when they love),
And that he could not bring his lips to say
What stirred within; for often ere he rode
I heard his steps along the terrace clang,
And, through the lattice looking, saw him take
Our Angelo, who stretched out both his arms,
And crowing strove with aimless hands to clutch
The nodding feather streaming from his cap;
While he would laugh, and with his black beard brush
The little rosy cheek, or with his lips
Catch the fat fingers of those dimpled hands;
The little creature, not the least afraid,
Would seize his beard, and scream his baby scream,
Or pat the cold steel plate above his heart.

Thus far it went—no farther. Love to him
Was like the glitter on that cold steel plate;
The gleam of pride—not the impassioned ray
That warms and glows through all the inner life.

I strove to recompense this aching want,
This thirsting for a sympathetic soul,
With thinking of my child and loving him.
But childish love is pure and innocent,
It cannot answer to the passion's call;
And hopeless, with a cruel load at heart,
I held my way unhappy and alone.

Beat as I would the bars that girt me round,
From my stern prison of necessity
No outlet opened save into the air;
And sitting sorrowing there, my wandering thoughts
Fled far and wild, and built ideal dreams,
And happy homes made beautiful by love;
Yet still the end was, dropping with a groan
Down to the same unhappy earth of fact,
More wretched for the joys that could not be.

I linger here—for here there came a change.
From this long distance, which is like to height,
I see the landscape of my life below.
There is its childhood's little garden plot,
Its weary marsh of stagnant womanhood,
Its one highway of duty—dusty, hard,
And leading nowhere. Eagle-like I plane
Above its drear Maremma solitudes,
Where there is ne'er a bird to sing of love;
And, rising far along the horizon's verge,
Behold the darkening storm come crowding up,
And know the lightnings that are hidden there.

Well, let me say it all at once: I loved.
My heart, long straining with its strong desires,
And hungered with a vague and craving want,
Snapt all at once its harsh and formal bands.
I stood alone within a clouded wood,
When sudden sunlight burst upon my path;
A scent of unknown flowers filled all the air—
The single cymbal with another clashed,
And wild triumphant music shook my thoughts.

We met—ah, fatal hour! we met and loved;
My heart rushed to him as the tideless lake,
Nearing the sheer precipitous abyss,
Rushes to ruin, and with one wild burst
Of storm and splendour down the rapids whirling,
Leaps, white with passion, to the lake below.
Vainly the trees along the shadowy shores,
Quivering with fear, cry to the rapids, "Stop!"
Vainly the hillsides strive to hold them back;
God's glorious rainbow o'er their terror glowing,
They rush to ruin, as we rushed to ours.

I was not guilty—guilty then of what?
Say, is the aloe guilty when it bursts
To its consummate flower, death though it bring?
If our two hearts, surcharged like wandering clouds
With love's intensest electricity,
Borne by the rushing winds from north and south,
Sent down the blasting lightnings when they struck
In heaven's broad dome, if without will they met,
Was it our fault? No; guilt is prearranged,
Is wilful—it demands consent at least.

How could we help it, if we met and loved?
If this be guilt, then nature is all guilt.
The love I bear my mother and my child,
The very hope of heaven itself, is guilt;
The very wind that blows, the eye that sees,
The heart that beats, are guilty, one and all.
What nature works in man and thing alike
Is innocent. I could not help but love.

My head is troubled by these swarming thoughts,
But I have need to speak, so let me speak.
Hark! is that he? Oh, save me from that man!
Save me! No, no, you shall not strike him here!
Stab at him through my heart, then, if you will!

Oh yes, I see. 'Twas but the jarring door,
The wind. Oh yes, I see—only the door.
'Tis past. I am not weak; let me go on.
No, dearest, no, no, no; let me go on.

The tears are in your eyes; I see the tears.
Mine are all wept away, years, years ago.

Oh keep your heart wide open; take therein
The floods that from grief's open sluices pour,
And pity, pity what you cannot change.
Give me your sympathy: I have not found
For such long years a patient pitying heart,
That now I feel that I must speak or die.
From fearful nightmares starting suddenly,
How sweet to tell the horrors we have passed,
Knowing they all have passed: so sweet to me
These dreadful passages of life to tell—
That never, never, will be wholly past.

We met—we loved. Oh, what a world there lies
In those four words! 'Twas in the summer days
When first we met—the last dear day of June,
That was the day—and love from bud to flower
Rushed with the sudden passion of our clime.
You know the shadowy laurel avenue,
Where, sheltered from the sun, we used to stroll
Those summer mornings when we both were girls;
And you remember, through the vista seen,
How the pomegranate blossoms glowed like fire

Against the old grey wall above the door;
'Twas there, beneath those flowers, I saw him first.
There, walking in the avenue alone,
I heard the Count, my husband, call my name,
And, looking round, just in the shadow there,
I saw him standing at my husband's side.
" Ginevra," said the Count, "my cousin here
Claims you as cousin too, since we are one.
I bring him here to you, for I am forced
(Against my will, I scarcely need to say)
To change a private joy for public care,
And leave him for a time in better hands.
My kinsman graciously excuses me
My forced departure for some hours; till then
You'll do the honours of our house for me,
And I alone shall suffer all the loss.
Ginevra, entertain our noble friend
With all that our poor villa can afford,
And piece its want out with the best of will."
So speaking, in his formal, courteous way,
He took his leave, and we were left alone.

You see he left us there; me fair and young—
I was so young then, and they called me fair—
He in the full completed prime of youth,
When all the blood runs riot in the veins,
And speaks from out the cheeks and lips and eyes.
Oh, Count, was this well done to leave us so?

He touched my hand, and bore it to his lips.
'Twas but a common courtesy; and yet
That touch ran through me like electric fire,
Thrilling my every nerve. At once his look,
By some peculiar mastery, seemed to seize
And to possess me, and I felt within
A tremulous movement in my thoughts, as when
The needle blindly struggles towards the pole.
He too was moved—his colour came and went;
We neither were at ease, we knew not why;
And so together, side by side, we strayed
Through the clipped alleys of the laurel walk,—
Or 'neath the shadow of the cypresses
We paused,—or, leaning on the parapet,

And gazing into purple distances,
Mechanically plucked from out its clefts
Some tiny flower or weed,—or, lingering near
The fountain's marble margin, idly watched
The gold-fish poising in its basin clear;
And while the babbling water gushed and dripped,
And reared its silver column in the sun,
And, over-weighted, dropped in pearls, our talk
Kept centring to our feelings from the range
Of outer facts with which it first began.
Oh golden morning! there you seem to float
Far off in memory, like a sun-flushed cloud,
With roseate heights, and tender dove-like shades;
No lightning in your bosom hid, no threat
Of passion, no remorse and death to come.
The air was faint with orange-flowers; the grove
Throbbed with the beats and thrills of nightingales
Hid in its covert green; along the wall
Flamed the pomegranate's fiery flowers; the rich
Rose clusters of the oleander bloomed
Soft in the violet shadows o'er them cast
By the grey villa. All the garden seemed

To swarm with happy life; the lizard stole
Along the fountain's marge, and stayed to gaze
With a shy confidence; the hawk-moth poised
Above the roses, thrust his slender trunk
Into their honeyed depths; on gauzy wings
The long green dragonfly in gleaming mail
Kept darting zigzag, hovering to and fro;
Hot bees were bustling in the flowers; with soft
And aimless flutter, painted butterflies
Hung drifting here and there like floating leaves,
Or rested on a weed to spread their wings.
All nature seemed in quiet happiness
To live and move,—and, thoughtless, without fear,
I shared that joy in harmony with it.
Swiftly the morning passed; and yet if hours
By inward change be counted, ere it went
Years had gone by, and life completely changed.

So as we talked, not owning to ourselves
The silent growth of love that was to bear
At last a poison-flower, a sudden voice
Startled us both. I knew it was the Count's,

And in my ear it sounded like a bell
That harshly scares us from a happy dream.
"Where are you?" cried he. "Oh, the Count!" I
said,
And started up, and saw him, cold and proud,
Turn the green corner of the laurel hedge,
And stand before us. With a formal speech
He broke the silence, offering excuse
That he had stayed away from us so long,
And asking pardon for disturbing us,
And then began to talk in stately way
Of what in council had been said and done,
As if this world were ours; and then, aghast,
I saw the chasm those short hours had rent
Between his soul and mine. Like some dull noise
I heard him talking as we walked along,
While all my thoughts were hurrying within
Wildly, and in my breast my fluttering heart
Was beating like a prisoned bird. At last
We reached the house, and to my room I rushed
For silence and for solitude. Once there,
I fell upon my bed, burst into tears,

And hid my face; for then I saw my fate—
Saw it rise up before me like a ghost.

Thus for a week our life went on: each day
The Count, made blind to everything by pride,
And by the vanity of ownership,
Left us along the garden walks to stroll,
Or in the house for hours alone to talk,
Not dreaming that *his* wife could dare to love;
And I was fearless too till every sense
Had drunk Love's sweet insidious poison in.
He was our guest; my husband day by day
Bade me be with him,—and no feigned excuse—
Excuse that was against my will, and yet
Feebly put forth, some barrier to rear
'Twixt love and duty—served to ope his eyes.
He blindly pushed us down that plane whereon
Vainly I sought for stay my course to stop.

How then resist? Duty is strong like will—
Passion like madness! I was wrenched away
From all that used to hold me; not a hand

Reached out to save me. Struggling thus alone,
If I but heard the Count's stern voice below
It seemed to freeze me; all my soul in arms
Started against him. Ah! no help was there.
Oh! how confess to him, and ask for help?

Then all my soul strained out to find a way
Back unto peace at least, if not to joy.
Glancing at all my life now left behind,
What was there to restrain me? Angelo,
My darling Angelo! His little arms,
Clasped close around my neck, should hold me back
From where my life was sweeping rapidly,
Yet all without my will. I grasped at this.
Alas! it had no strength to save me then.

We walk along with such a fearless trust
Through unknown dangers; yet our death may lie
Within one drop of poison that the ring
On a friend's hand may hold. One whispered word
May shake the avalanche down upon our head—
One moment more or less destroy or save.

The whole vast world without, and that within,
Turn on a pivot's point, and, jarred from that,
Both universes into ruin rush.

'Twas thus with me: before, at least, secure,
And if not happy yet without a fear;
And now a word, an hour, had changed my life.
A word? an hour? Ah, no! for years and years,
The train within my being had been laid.
My cruel disappointments, broken hopes,
And crushed desires—a black and ugly mass,
Were powder to a single spark of love;
Oh! bid *that*, touched by fire, not to explode.

Yet ah the bliss of loving and the pain!
For I had never lived until I loved;
Yet evermore a terror 'neath the bliss
Constrained it, like some fearful undertow,
That dimples the smooth river's sunlit brim,
To drag the stoutest swimmer down to death.

On, on, my thoughts went—there was no return;
One backward step no soul can ever take.

My life thus far had been as dull and dead
As a deserted eagle's nest that hangs
In the black shadow of an Alpine cliff—
The shining saint-like heights too far above,
The humble valley's peace too far below.
Wild, gusty, furious, with a moment's wrench
The hurricane of passion swept me down,
And, swirled along by fierce tumultuous thoughts,
Torn from the past, the future all unknown,
I hovered 'twixt the sky and the abyss.

Broken in body, spent in soul, at last
I gave myself to Fate. Do what thou wilt,
I cried, my strength is gone—I yield to thee;
Crush me or save me, I can strive no more.
Thus all my sudden passion cried in me;
But better thoughts at last with time arose.
Perhaps, perhaps, I said, he does not love;
'Twas my own heart that shone upon his face.
Oh! if it be so, all may yet be safe,
And I will hide my secret from his eyes,
And only act and speak as friends may do.

Yes, let me struggle for a while, and then,
This visit over, I can die alone.

Oh, vain, vain, vain! day after day I saw
That love consumed his heart as well as mine.
Fate set its face against us from the first.
Day after day we could not help but meet.
All stay, all resolution formed between
Our constant meetings, when we met, gave way.
We could not dash the cup down from our lips,
Despite the poison that we knew it held.
He strove to make excuses to depart,
But still he lingered; and in constant fear
Each that our love might blaze into an act,
Or that a word might make our love a crime,
Life rushed along in terrible pretence.

But oh, how dear for all their pain they were,
Those blissful, fearful days! Left all alone—
For every morning went the Count to town,
And Guido sometimes would not brook excuse—
We ranged the garden 'neath the laurel shade;

Or, where the waving trumpet-flowers outstretched
Their red tubes, shaken by the buried bees,
We sat together, hiding as we could
With veil of words the life that glowed beneath.
But even the widest circle of our talk,
Strive as we would, drew to one centre—love;
And there he told me of his early days,
And all his early hopes and joys and pains,
And painted his ideal of a life:
Oh what a life it was!—but not for us.
And then upon the pure stream of his voice
Such songs of poets slid into my soul;
So sad, too, that they brought the brimming tears:
And oft like poplars quivering in the breeze
We trembled with the joy we dared not own;
And oft we started up on some excuse,
And left each other when we could not bear
Our overburden—I to weep and pray,
And he, dear heart, I think, to do the same.

One day we talked of rings as there we sat—
Of Cleopatra's she dissolved and drank,

And of Morone's, whence a devil spake.
And I by chance upon my finger wore
This which I wear for ever now, when he,
Taking my hand and looking at this ring—
"Give it to me," said, jesting; "I will swear
I'll ne'er dissolve it Cleopatra-like;
'Tis but a little thing—for friendship's sake
Give it to me, and when I look at it
I'll hear an angel, not a devil, speak."
I answered, bantering, "Shall I give it you
To put upon the first fair lady's hand
You fall in love with, or to boast to men
Here is a trophy? No, Sir Guido, no;
You think you'll keep it, but I know you men."

"Now Heaven be witness, never shall it leave
This hand of mine if you'll but put it there.
Shall I make oath? Then hear me, cousin mine:
I swear to keep the ring while life shall last;
And lest it fall into unworthy hands,
Dying I'll send it back to you again.
So when it comes without me, pray for me."

"So serious," answered I; "then take the ring,
And we shall see if man can keep his oath."

I knew the inward struggle—loved him more
The more I saw him fight against his Fate.
His acts were only common courtesies,
And ne'er a word betrayed what throbbed within.
Yet were words wanting? Ah! we read too well
The passion burning in each other's face,
That would not be concealed howe'er we strove.
If but my scarf would touch his hand, a flush
Went like a thrill of music o'er his face,
And subtle tones transfigured common words.
At last, convulsed, in one wild hour he told
His desperate love: he flung him at my feet;
His heart cried out, "Oh kill me where I lie,
Here where I kiss the print your foot has made
Upon the grass! Oh, dearer here to die,
Knowing you love me, than to weary out
The death of life afar from you, my heaven!"

Oh God forgive me! but I loved him so,

That honour for an instant's flash went out.
All my resolves burst like a broken dam,
And "Up!" I wildly cried; "not at my feet,
Here on my heart thy place—here on my heart!"

Then all was over; once those rash words said,
We never more could meet as we had met;
Our souls gazed at each other face to face,
And saw in that one look that all was lost.

Yet do not think that guilt then stained our souls.
Guilty of love we were—of nothing else;
But thus to see him in his agony
Was worse than death. I could not even say,
Go!—for I feared some sudden desperate end.
I strove to soothe him—*I* to soothe him—*I*
Who burned with fiercer flames than martyrs know:
I uttered bitter comfort—stretched my hand
To that poor sufferer burning at my side.
And when he cried, "Oh God, forgive me now!
And you, Ginevra—oh my fate, my fate!"
Though death griped at my heart, and passion's self

Struggled with duty for my very life,
"Patience," I cried, "and God will help us both!
Why should we suffer thus who do no wrong?"
Then starting up, and pacing to and fro,
He madly struck his forehead, crying out,
"Oh! were there only something to be done,
Not something to be suffered, to be borne."
Or bitter accusations of himself
He uttered, saying, "I have broken faith—
Broken my oath to which I swore myself—
And all is over now. No more dear days,
When I at least can see and feel you near.
'Tis over now—ah yes!—all over now.
I feel the fire-sword whirling round my head
To drive me from you, out of Paradise."

"Oh, say not so—we cannot help our love;
And though we may not meet as now we meet,
A way may yet be shown we cannot see.
Now go—oh leave me, Guido, for my heart
Is breaking, and there's no more life for me!"
I, longing to console his tortured heart,

And scarcely knowing what I meant myself,
Uttered these words, and tore myself away.

Look at me now—see how I tremble now;
Think if the memory can tear me thus,
What agony I suffered in that hour.
Oh dearest Guido—dearest, dearest heart—
It was not sin to love a soul like yours,
For you were made to win and wear the best,—
Not one like me. O cruel, cursed Fate,
Why did I ever live beyond that hour!

How strange the world looked as I wandered back
Into the palace! what a broken heart
The nightingale had then, that in the grove
Throbbed into song! what spirit-voices sighed
And mourned amid the cypresses! how dear
The soft blue sky looked, and how peaceful too,
As if to soothe me! Even the house looked strange,
Like some new place I had not seen before.
I walked as in a dream; I could not bear

The common things—the common speech of life;
All that I asked was solitude and tears.
For two long weary days I kept my room,
Broken in body, sick to death at heart;
And as I lay all prostrate on the floor
After a sudden agony of tears—
One of those bursts with which the tortured soul
Relieves its passion—came a sudden knock;
It seemed as Death were knocking at the door.
In walked the Count; I started to my feet,
I strove to gather my disordered dress,
And smooth my face, and wipe away my tears.
My soul revolted, and I saw his eye,
Dread as a basilisk's, upon me rest;
A strange expression, never seen before,
Was brandished there. He said, "'Tis very strange
Guido is gone, and leaves a note behind,
More like a riddle than a note; and you——"
His eyes filled up the gap his speech had left.
"Is Guido gone?" I said; I could no more.
For as he spoke these words the whole world seemed
To slip beneath me—all my world was gone.

Such weight as this upon the suffering heart
Will show itself, however we may strive;
And in an instant all my secret lay
Before his gaze, as when a sudden wind
Blows wide the closed leaves of a fatal book.
He read the page—he never spoke a word,
But paused a moment, read it up and down,
Then turned and left me, terribly alone.

The evening came to that distracting day—
The evening comes at last to every day.
Exhausted, in a hopeless lull of life,
I watched the burning sunset slowly fade,
Till all the clouds from rose had turned to pearl,
And in the sky the silver splendour shone
Of perfect moonlight; on the shadowy trees
The moon looked pitying down, as if it sought
To give me consolation from above,
And Nature seemed to whisper me, "Come forth."
I could not rest, and down the dappled path,
Where light and shade their strange mosaic wove,
Through the old laurels took my aimless way.

There, half as in a dream, I wandered on,
And, weeping, praying, strove to ease my pain.
The laurels murmured, "Ah, we pity you!"
The fountain babbled, "Ah, unhappy one!"
The nightingale sang out, "My heart, my heart!
And all things seemed to weep and pray with me.
Hark! did I hear a step upon the grass?
Was that a ghost I saw amid the trees?
Or Guido's self? or was my brain disturbed?
No; in the shadow there was Guido's self;—
"Oh, heaven!" I cried; "Oh Guido! are you here?
Fly—fly at once! Oh! wherefore are you here?"

He rushed to me—and, oh! that glorious face—
So haggard, worn, and ravaged with its woe—
How changed it seemed since I had seen it last!
I cried out, "Go!" but all within me strained
To clasp him, own him, cling around his neck;—
I cried out, "Go!" as one in madness cries,
"Save me!" and leaps to death in an abyss.
A thousand prayers and longings, flinging out
Their grasping hands, reached forward after him,

And love, with all its sails blown sudden out,
Strained at the cable of my weakened will.

"I go—I go!" he cried; "I but returned
To kiss again the ground your feet had pressed,
To watch your far light in the window shine,
To see your wandering shadow there—and then
Plunge back into my desolated world.
But God hath sent you here—He pitied me—
He saw me grovelling like a tortured worm
Crushed in the grass, and reached His hand to me.
I see you, hear you, touch you, once again—
And can it only be to say, Adieu?"

"Oh, Guido, fly!" I cried, "for I am weak;
Fly from me if you love me—I am weak."

He stood a moment, wrestling with himself,
I gazing at him; then a sudden power
Seemed to transform him. "No! I will not go!
'Tis all in vain—I cannot, will not, go!
Once I have fled, fleeing from joy, from hope,

From life, from heaven. Whose hand then drew me
back?
Who led your footsteps here? Whose hand, I say?
Fate gives you me at last! Fate makes you mine!—
Life is but mockery bereft of you.
Fly, fly with me, and in some distant spot,
Hid from the world, we may be happy yet."

His passion took me as a mighty gale,
Crowded with thunder, drives upon the elm,
Till all its straining branches groaning cry,
And toss their helpless turbulence of leaves,
And fall at last in one despairing crash;
So, bearing down resolve, and blowing wild
All my disordered thoughts, his passion came.
Defenceless—weakened, both in strength and will—
Against this new arousing from within,
Against this new appealing from without,
Vain was resistance: I was in his arms!
He seemed to hold me there by heaven's own right.
The world was for a moment all forgot—
The world! I had the world there in my arms!

Nothing then seemed so right, so pure, as love.
Yes, I was his, irrevocably his—
Come heaven, come hell, irrevocably his!

'Twas but a moment's madness seized me then—
A blank of reason such as comes to one
Who, clinging for his life to some sheer cliff,
Feels his strength going and his senses swim,
And death come swooping down, and longs to drop
And end it all: so, for a moment's space,
I swooned; and then God's voice within me cried
"No!" and uprising, and beneath my feet,
Trampling my love, with gesture stern and quick
I pushed the dearest thing in life away.
I know not whence I got the strength I had:
Some hand—whose hand but God's?—uplifted me.
From duty's height I saw the war below
Of my own passions as they were not mine.
"Oh, Guido, shame!" I cried; "I am not yours—
You mine—but only as we both are God's."

That was a height to die on—but I lived;
Death always comes too early or too late.

Life had its claims for penance—so I lived;
Nor will I murmur more—perhaps 'tis just.

Those words of mine, like an electric flash,
Broke the strained storm of madness in his sky,
And the great shadow and the rain came down—
Shadow as of despair,—yet nobler far,
Dearer in his despair than in his pride.
The prayers he uttered for forgiveness then
Were worst of all to bear,—I hear them still
Ring in my ears; that face of his I see
Streaming with tears; and those contorted hands,
Grasping the air, or torturing themselves,
Or wildly flung to heaven, still implore
Our dear Madonna's blessing on my head—
What are so terrible as manhood's tears?
At last we parted—Heaven alone knows how—
And all was over; I was left alone—
Alone? I never more could be alone.

The owl screamed near us in the cypress-tree.
Half-dead, I saw him go as in a dream,

And heard his footsteps down the gravel die.
The gate swung with a clang—"My God! my God!
Help me!" I moaned; only the owl replied.

I dropped upon the seat—I hid my face
Within my hands; all, all the world seemed gone.
I longed to rise and call him back again,
But my feet failed me. There I sat alone,
Like him, half-marble, in the Arabian tale,
Charmed by foul magic, when a distant sound
Smote on my ears. It was the clash of steel.
I started up, with sudden terror fired,
And towards the gate I rushed. My flying feet
Grating upon the gravel hushed the sound.
I stopped to listen; there it was again—
And voices, too—oh, Heaven! Again I fled;
Again I only heard my grating steps.
I gained the gate—I listened—all was still.
The moon broke out behind a cloud, and smote
The pale broad palace front, where nothing stirred;
Only the tall dark cypresses made moan,
And the hoar olives seemed like ghosts to flee

Across the hillside, where a whisper ran—
"'Twas but his sword that jangled on the ground,"
I said; "for see, how all is hushed to rest!
Poor heart of mine, that trembles at a breath,
Be calm again, and cast your fear away.
But ah! the wretched days before we meet—
The sunless days—yet we shall meet again."

The far-off bell upon the Campo tower
Struck twelve as up the terrace-steps I went:
I paused to soothe me with the landscape there.
The shadowy earth was turning in its sleep,
And winds were whispering over it like dreams;
The luminous sky was listening overhead
With its full moon, and few great throbbing stars—
One drowsing like a sick man, sad and dark;
One watching like a spirit, pure and bright.
All the damp shadow clinging to the ground,
Shook, with innumerable tiny bells,
Rung by the grilli. In the distant pools
Frogs trilled and gurgled; every now and then
The plaintive hooting of the owl was heard

Calling her owlets 'mid the cypresses;
Near by, the fountain spilled, and far away
The contadino's watchdog bayed and barked;—
Yet all these sounds were soothed and harmonised
By night's weird hand; and as I listening stood,
Leaning against the columned balustrade,
By aloe vases crowned, my turbulent thoughts
Were calmed—I looked into the sky, and prayed.

The Count not yet returned? Then all is safe.
I took my lamp, and up the marble stairs
My heart jarred to the echoes of my feet;
A swinging shutter down the corridor
So startled me, I nearly dropped the light.
Was I possessed? Almost it seemed to me
As if a spirit wandered in my room.
I could not feel alone there; through my hair
Ran shudders, and a creeping o'er my flesh.
I searched the room, but there was nothing there.
My silk dress as it rustled on the chair
Scared me; the creeping curtain scared me too,
And, daring not to move a hand or foot,

I listened trembling. There was nothing there,
Unless it was a ghost I could not see.
My nerves were all ajar—the buzzing flies
I could not bear; but worse than all, the sense
Of something—some one—there within my room.

My lamp extinguished, into bed I crept,
And hid me 'neath the sheets, and wept such tears,
And prayed such prayers, as desperate creatures pray.

All night the Count returned not to his room;
No step I heard, though long I lay awake.
'Twas strange—'twas not his wont. What could it mean?
Troubled and overworn, at last I slept,
Haunted by dreams that ran in dreadful ruts
With weary sameness through my aching brain.

The morning came—the Count was absent still.
Haunted by vague and agitating fears,
I waited almost as one waits for death;
And after torturing hours, that seemed like years
To my strained sense, I heard a step. The door

Turned on its hinges, and there stood the Count:
A cold false smile was on his lips; his look
Was strangely calm—not real. Those hard eyes
Betrayed a purpose that belied the lips—
Belied the courtesy so overstrained.
"I fear you did not look for me," he said;
"Nor have I tidings that can give you joy.
I came a sacred promise to fulfil—
One I could not refuse; and, as you know,
All promises are sacred that I make.
I promised Guido in your hands to place
This, which he took from you, and now returns."
Saying these words, he on the table laid
My ring—the ring that I to Guido gave.

Oh what an awful light was in his eyes!
Oh what a devil's smile was on his lips!
As there he stood, still as a marble man.
My heart stopped beating, numbed by hideous fear—
There was a silence terrible as death:
The terror stunned me, and I could not speak.
Speak!—no, I could not feel. There was no sense

In anything; my very blood was ice.
I could not tell an instant if 'twere he,
My husband, standing there—or if 'twere I
Who stood before him. Then I reeled and fell—
I did not swoon; I dropped into my chair
Like one knocked down with an invisible blow.
He moved not; but an instant after said,
Slowly—his words like to the first great drops
That tell the storm is coming, forced between
His thin white lips—"Your cousin, madam, 's gone;
That ring he sent; he said you'd understand."

"Oh God! God! God!" I cried, "it is not true!
What do you mean by *gone?*—speak, speak to me!
Say 'tis but a dream—oh, tell me 'tis a jest;
Oh yes, it is a jest, or you'd not smile."

"Jest! Do I look, then, like a jesting man?
Madam, your lover, after your last kiss,
Wiped my dishonour out with his heart's blood.
He knew the wrong he did—saw for us two,
After such scene as that of yesternight

The world was narrow; so he bravely fell
To expiate the cruel wrong he did."

"Dead! dead! oh God! oh Guido!—oh my God!"
Something like this I shrieked, and moaned and fell.

Slowly at last, and after hours, returned
My scattered senses; and long days went by—
Eternities of utter reckless woe;
With bursts of agony and burning tears,
And daring hopes that all might be a lie,
Mingled with prayers, half-raving, after death.
I almost looked on God, who sent the sun,
As heartless. Why should flowers and blossoms grow?
Why should all nature look so bright and fair,
And birds be singing, and the world be gay,
Except to mock me with its happiness?
Then came as strong revulsions; ne'er before
Knew I what wickedness was in my heart.
In the excited tumult of my brain
I could not see the right—I felt the wrong;
The great black hand of death before my eyes

Darkened my conscience. Oh such savage thoughts
As then roused up and ravaged in the dark!
I could not calm myself to right resolve;
Forgiveness seemed impossible to reach—
Starlike; but vengeance like a devil stood
And offered me its sword, and tempted me,
And would not let me hear the angel's voice;
But still that sweet persistent voice within
Kept calling, till it conquered all at last.
I would forgive and crave forgiveness too.

So governing the wild and cruel thoughts
That growled for vengeance, I awaited him.

At last he came; cold, stern, and dignified,
That mask of honour came into my room.
"Well, sir," I said, "you see me broken, crushed,
Ruined—a helpless, wretched, tortured thing.
If I have been imprudent, heedless, wrong—
For so I was—you are at least avenged:
Your foot has trodden on my erring heart,
As if I were a worm upon your path.

See how it writhes! Oh, sir! are you content?
May God forgive you for your cruel wrong,
And help me in my struggles to forgive."

"Forgiveness! wrong! Your choice of terms is strange.
I crave forgiveness? Let that task be yours;
Ask it upon your knees of God and me.
Wrong? There's no wrong but what belongs to you.
Though I regret what honour made me do,
I did my duty; had you done but yours,
All would be smooth and happy as it was."

"Happy! oh when was happiness for me,
Or when again shall happiness be mine?
Happy? Where's Guido? Tell me that he lives;
You could not speak of happiness to me,
If you had killed him for a fault of mine.
Say 'twas a jest you used to frighten me—
Say this, and I will never see him more.
Oh, I will do my duty with a smile,
Bless you, and crave forgiveness—do your will,
And fetch and carry for you like a dog."

"Your duty! Yes, I think you will indeed;
I shall take heed of that. Not see him more?
For that, too, my security is good,—
I am not used to do my work by halves."

Then the desire of death—my love—his blood—
The pride and cruel calmness of the Count—
The taunting smile with which he looked at me,
Roused all the evil passions I had quelled.
All things will turn when tortured, and I cried,

"Oh, kill me then, too, with the self-same sword!
Oh how I scorn you! let your passion speak!
I loved him—loved him—loved him, do you hear?
Out with your sword if you have any heart!
Kill me in pity, since you've murdered him."

"Murdered! no, hand to hand and point to point,
With every chance, he fell; he owned his wrong.
There lives no man in whom a single spark
Of honour burns, that had not done as I;
I gave him every chance—he lost, and fell."

"I say I loved him better than my life."

"For that I killed him. He will love no more."

"He loves me still,—above as I below.
Oh, I am his, he mine, beyond your power—
You do but part us for a little space;
And in the future, after life is o'er,
My soul shall rush to clasp him closer there,
Than could my human arms when here on earth."

"Ginevra! do you heed the words you use?
You dared not more than let him speak of love?
Silent? You leave me then to think the worst."

"Think what you choose—do what you choose—I loathe
Alike your foul thoughts and your cruel act."

"Then my name's blasted and my honour stained,
And I have blazoned it to all the world."

"Your name, your honour stained! Ay, so it is!

But not by me, not by my guiltless love—
Guiltless, though fatal. Not a thought for mine
Held back your hand. Blindly, through Guido's life,
My honour too you struck at, blazoning
To the wide world that ours was guilty love."

"I would to God that none of this had been!"

"Nor had it ever been, except for you.
You bound the life of Guido unto mine;
You brought him here, you tempted both of us,
And now affect surprise to find we loved.
Careless of others, centred in yourself,
You could not claim a love you never gave.
What debt beyond allegiance did I owe?"

"What have you ever asked that was not given?
My wealth, my name, my rank, my house, were yours,
And in return you stain my ancient name,
For all the world to point its finger at.
A husband's duty I at least have done—
And honestly, I think. Have you a wife's?"

"I have done all I could. O pity me,
And do not urge a desperate creature on.
Think what I suffer. Pity and forgive.
I own my fault—I ask you to forgive.
I was not all to blame; you, too, must bear
A portion of the wrong—at least be just."

"What was my fault?—what portion of the wrong?
Be just, you say. Of course I shall be just."

"For this, at least, you were to blame: you swore
To love, to honour, and to cherish me
For all my life. How did you keep your oath?
You left me all defenceless to be prey
To solitude, to idleness, to chance.
What have I asked, you say, that was not given?
Love, love—'twas that I craved; not title, wealth,
Or name, but daily acts of tenderness.
God knows how long I strove, how earnestly,
To patch with duty the great gap of love.
It would not do; my nature yearned for more.
Well! give a starving wretch upon a wreck

A golden florin when he cries for bread!
Will it suffice? No; 'tis mere mockery.
And so were all your vaunted gifts—no flower
In the chill ruin of my hopes you left;
By heartless duties, dull routine, you froze
My eager nature;—Sudden, like the breath
Of southern spring, with all its roses in it,
Love breathed across me—all my life broke up
Like some great river's ice at touch of spring,
And I was borne in one great burst away."

"Fine phrases—pretty pictures—nothing more!
And did no thought of honour hold you back?"

"Honour! ah, honour! wretched mud-built dam!
Could that avail to stem the swollen stream?
Acts, yes—but nothing else. If I was stunned,
Aghast, to feel the formless dreams of love
Take passion's tyrannous and threatening shape,
What help was there? Oh no, you cannot see!
As well the stagnant pool, all creamed with green,
Sees why the torrent, shaking its white spray,

And mad with all the tumult of its course,
Can pause not on the brink of the abyss.
Who put temptation in my very path?
You—you who should have held me—dragged me down.
What right had you to leave me to such chance?"

"It was a fault, I see—it was a fault.
But who could think you such a worthless thing
As take the first fair apple Satan gave?
Curse, curse the hour, oh woman, when you did!
His blood is on your hands, and not on mine;
Wipe it away, then, if you can, with words.
You knew the path you trod led straight to death.
You ventured all—your fame—my name—his life—
For what?—to satisfy a moment's whim.
You, like a child that sees a pretty flower
That's caught a holding down a precipice,
Dared everything to wear it on your breast.
Your foot slipped—why, of course, of course it slipped,
Weak woman-brain—and down to death you went.
Go, wet his grave now with your idle tears;
Will they bring back the life you sacrificed?"

"Oh, had you loved me this had never been!
I sought a flower?—I sought it for a whim?—
Ah, no! Love tempted with a ripe, rare fruit,
A starving creature, who refused the gift,
And laid her down to die for honour's sake.
I did refuse it—yes, you know I did.
Nay, look not on me with that devil's smile;
It makes me almost hate you. Not alone
'Tis love you lack, but pity, but remorse,
But conscience! Never shall that hand again,
Stained by his blood, touch mine—'tis widowed now.
Nay, play not with your poniard,—out with it!
Strike! there's no thing that wants its death so much.
Strike! here I stand. Strike as you struck at him!
Strike, soul of honour! Ah! you calculate—
Your cold blood cannot stir. I see your eyes—
They are arranging. No, it will not do
To trust an impulse—you must think it out.
Oh be a man for once, and dare to strike!"

I know I touched him—touched him to the quick;
I saw it in the twitching of his hands:

Yet there he stood, with his contemptuous smile
That maddened every feeling. All at once
A sudden cord within my brain gave way;
The pulse's hammers in my temples beat.
The last thing that I saw was his black eyes—
I see them still; then with a cymbal's clash
The sunlight shattered to a myriad sparks;
And what became of me, God only knows.

When to my senses I again returned,
I felt myself borne rapidly along
In a horse-litter. To my brain confused
All the last scene came back again to me;
For every word had burned into my soul,
But not as aught that really had been,
Only an ugly, wild, and hideous dream;
And mixed with it a thousand horrid thoughts,
That seemed as real as the actual were.

I tore the curtains open, and looked out;
I asked no question—for, had I been dead,
I had not cared less what they did with me;

Life had gone by—'twas just the same as death
When on the floor I fainted. Now I woke
Into a kind of life that was not mine:
The night itself was weird, like all my thoughts;
Strange clouds piled wildly all along the sky,
And, hurrying to and fro, shut out its light.
The earth was swallowed up in heavy dark;
Low thunder growled; at sudden fits the sky
Winked with white lightnings 'neath the black low brows
Of clouds along the horizon, and glared out
Across the world, and showed the trembling trees
Ghastly against it; then the black again
Swallowed the world up, and I heard great drops
Beat on the leaves. From one low threatening cloud,
That rose to meet us, leaped out suddenly
A crinkled snake of fire, then darted in;
And thunder trampled with tumultuous roar:
Or was it rather that the angel flashed
His sword of jagged fire that drove me out
From Paradise, and God's dread voice I heard
Behind the cloud to threaten my lost soul?

All worn and weak, and shattered in my nerves,
I could not bear the sight; and back I fell,
Only half-conscious; and I seemed to feel
The horse's hoofs keep beating on my brain;
And now and then a startling thunder-peal.
All sense of time was gone. At last I slept,
Or swooned—for all things faded into blank.

What happened afterwards I do not know:
What first I saw, when any sense came back,
Were these four walls, and my old Rosa's face
Looking on mine with pity as she bent
Above my pillow, and I heard her say,
"Oh blessed Virgin!—see, she wakes at last!"

From that day forward, now for ten long years,
Here is my prison; here the sad sun shines,
But never shines for me a loving smile.
His face, that would have made the dreariest spot
A paradise, has gone beyond the world;
And he that spared my life and crushed my heart,
Since that last day has never looked on me.

This is his vengeance—he has hid me here,
Beyond all hope of change, to waste away,
Unloved, uncared for, like an outcast thing,
To suck the fever's pestilential air,
And see the sad Maremma's lonely waste,
And hear the beating of the restless sea;
While in its marsh of drear monotony,
Life breeds its poison-thoughts, and wastes, and rots.

Ah death! death! death! how have I prayed for
you!
You take the happy, fold them in your arms,
And kiss them to the slumber of the blest;
But from my path in scorn you turn aside.

Oh! think what years they've buried me alive
In this drear villa all alone, alone;
Long days alone—long, long black nights alone;
And I was never over-brave, you know.
Imprisoned with the recollected past,
Without a future, weak with illness too,
I grew to fear my very self (what more

Is there on earth to fear?) My eyes looked strange
In these blear mirrors. Through the noiseless night
Often I lay and shuddered in the blank
Dead waste of darkness, while my great square room
Seemed like a shadowy tomb to shut me in;
And all the darkness weighed on me like death.
Then, straining out into the empty void,
My eyes made globes of pale electric fire,
That swelled and faded into globes of black,
And hours I used to watch them come and go.
Nor was it better, when the sad-faced moon
Mocked at me in its far-off silentness.
Daylight at times was worse: the blazing sun
Flashed on the sea that shook its burning plates,
And through the shutters' slightest chink peered in
To crawl and quiver on the ceiling there.
Hide as I would, I felt the fierce white noon
Seethe round the house and eat into my room,
In busy silence prying to and fro
As if in search of me. All was so still,
Despite the shrill cicale's saw without,
And maddening burring buzz of flies within.

Even the melancholy wash of waves
Broke not the silence—nor the voiceless pines,
That always whispered though the breezes slept.
Only my echoing feet in the great hall,
As to and fro I paced, broke the dead calm.
And thus the dreary weary days passed by—
No duty to be done, no life to live;
For surely what I lived was never life.

Was it, then, strange I lost my head at last?
But that is over now, and passed away;
'Tis only when the fever comes, my thoughts
Dance to discordant music. Then at times
They seem to gather to a single point,
And, widening, whirl and whirl with buzz and din
Till all the world swarms like a spinning mass,
And down, down, down, as in a maelstrom's cone,
My spirit, worn with struggle, madly goes,
Like a lost ship, and all becomes a blank.
Thus, helpless, down the vortex borne I reel,
Until, the fever gone, a wretched wreck
Flung out I find me on the shores of life.

Ah ! dearest, Joy unto the spirit is
What light is to the flowers—no colour else.
Joy is the voice of Good—the voice of God;
And when my heart was barren of all joy,
It sicklied like a plant derived of light.

I have been mad—who would not have been mad?—
And hideous visions have obscured my soul.
Long time some dreadful thing I had to hide—
Some vague and dreadful thing, without a name.
Here in the walls it lived and peeped at me;
Long lonely nights kept whispering at my blinds,
Leaped out of flowers when I had gathered them,
And placed them on my bosom; with its laugh
Scared the still noon, and would not let me rest.

That went at last, though sometimes it returns;
And though I know 'tis all a hideous dream,
Yet through my tangled thoughts so long it trod,
It wore a track there that will never go.
And for a moment often it returns,
And I seem mad because I speak of it;

But do not think I'm mad, or not more mad
Than any human creature kept so long
In this wild place alone, and with such things.

When all is dark, on dismal gusty nights,
Ghosts wander all around this lonely house,
And smothered groans and stifled shrieks I hear,
That mingle with the beating of the sea.
Sometimes the giant rafters creak and strain,
And overhead there rush tumultuous feet,—
Or slow and heavy steps, with clank of spurs,
Stride nearer, nearer up the sounding stairs,
Till, wild with fear, I see the shaking door
Swing open slowly on its creaking hinge,
To let some ghastly unseen horror in.
But most I dread to pass that banquet-hall,
Where rotting cobwebs flaunt their dusky flags
From its black beams—or up the chimney suck,
When through its sooty throat the tempest roars;
For then fierce spirits seem to hold carouse,
And with their hideous revelry and laugh
Jar the loose windows; and the shields and swords

Clang on the walls as if they longed for blood.
All this, you'll say, is fancy. Live here, then,
Through the drear winter all alone, alone,
With these wild terrors grasping after you.
Oh God ! we were not made to live alone—
We all go mad if we are left alone.

My child, too. Ah, my little Angelo !
Where are you now ?—Oh, tell me where he is !
That little rosy face that hid itself
Around my neck with both hands clasping it.
Oh, such long years since I have felt those hands !
How cruel, cruel, from my arms to tear
The only thing he gave me that I loved !
How many nights I've dreamed that he was here ;
How many mornings waked, and wept, and wailed
To find me here alone—more desolate
For the sweet dream that came and went at will.
He has grown up to boyhood now, I know.
He has forgotten me—my name's a word
Banned to his lips—he knows not that I live ;
Yet in my memory how alive he is,

A baby blessing—with those four white teeth
Gleaming beneath the little sudden smile,
The dimpled elbows and the rosy feet
Never at rest—the unformed chirping words
Like a bird's language—all the many ways
With which he crept into my very heart.
Oh! 'twas a cruel act, a wicked act,
To tear him from me. How has he grown up
Without a mother's love? Oh, justice, Count!—
Your justice—did it soothe his little cries?
He has your name, but not, I pray, your heart.
One drop of love is worth a well of pride.

Why should I cling to life? A hundred times
I've pressed this dagger to my throbbing heart—
A hundred times I have not dared to strike;
And yet how blest a thing were death to me!

I think at last my time is drawing near.
Ah, heaven! I hope 'tis drawing near at last,
I have so suffered. Even he would strike
That sword of his in justice to my heart.

He would relent, I think—I hope he would—
Could he but see me now; even he to whom
Mercy is slow to whisper, would forgive.
Justice so strained is vengeance, nothing more—
All has so changed, and I was wrong, I know.
Yet no! What do I say?—he, he forgive?
Never! They only can forgive who love.
He knows not pity for an erring heart.
Justice and honour:—these two are his gods;
To them alone his sacrifice is given.

Why do I rail at him? Do I forgive?
Am I so free from blot? Was I all right?
Ah no! we both were wrong, we all were wrong!
In these long days reviewing all the past
I know and feel how very wrong we were.
I plainly see (the passion cleared away)
No fit excuse for Guido and for me.
Tempted we were beyond our human power;
But after marriage-vows, if love come in,
Its torture we must own and bear—like death.
My punishment is just—his too, perhaps;

But man is not to blame as woman is.
Mine was the greater fault: I led him on,
He loved me so; and he was all alone.

I should have checked his love when it began;
I should have bade him go, and turned my thoughts
To household duties; but I played with fire,
And mine the fault that both were sacrificed.
The Count was not so wrong as then he seemed;
And from his view his deed was justified.
And he has suffered too—and I forgive—
Yes, as I need forgiveness, I forgive.
And so I pray for all, even for the Count;
And, looking forward, fix my eyes above,
To meet my Guido when this life is past.

What matters it?—a few short years, or months,
Or weeks, perhaps—or even a few more days—
And I shall be with him, where love's no crime,
And God, who sees the heart, will pity me.
Oh, yes! God's law is tenderer than man's.
He is not only just—but pity too,

And love, unbounded love, He has for all;
And He will make all smooth and right at last.
So let me weep upon your breast, dear friend—
My only solace for these long long years.
God will remember you for this—His arm
Is long—His memory will never fail;
And He will make all smooth and right at last.

PADRE BANDELLI PROSES

TO

THE DUKE LUDOVICO SFORZA

ABOUT

LEONARDO DA VINCI.

Two steps, your Highness—let me go before,
And let some light down this dark corridor—
Ser Leonardo keeps the only key
To the main entrance here so jealously,
That we must creep in at this secret door
If we his great Cenacolo would see.

The work shows talent—*that* I must confess;
The heads, too, are expressive, every one;
But, with his idling and fastidiousness,
I fear his picture never will be done.

I pray your Highness' pardon for my zeal—
Were it for sake of us poor Frati here,
Despite the inconvenience we must feel,
Kept out from our refectory now a year
And eight long months (though that, of course, for us
Whose lives to mortify the flesh are vowed,
Even to mention seems ridiculous)—
Were it for us alone, we all had bowed;
But when we see your Highness set at nought,
Who ordered this great picture to be wrought,
We cannot rest content, for well we know
What duty to our gracious prince we owe.
And I, the unworthy prior here—(God knows
How much I feel my own unworthiness,
But *He* hath power the meanest hand to bless;
And if our convent prospereth in aught,
Not mine, but *His*, the praise, who all bestows)—
But being the prior and the head, and so
Charged to your interests and theirs, I thought
My duty—an unpleasant one, in sooth—
Was simply to acquaint you with the truth,

And pray your Highness with your eyes to see
How things go on in our refectory;
And then your Highness only has to say
Unto this painter—"Sir, no more delay!"
And all is done, for you he must obey.

'Tis twenty months since first upon the wall
This Leonardo smoothed his plaster—then
He spent two months ere he began to scrawl
His figures, which were scarcely outlined, when
Some new fit seized him, and he spoilt them all.
As he began the first month that he came,
So he went on, month after month the same.
At times, when he had worked from morn to night
For weeks and weeks on some apostle's head,
In one hour, as it were from sudden spite,
He'd wipe it out. When I remonstrated,
Saying, "Ser Leonardo, you erase
More than you leave—that's not the way to paint;
Before you finish we shall all be dead;"
Smiling he turns (he has a pleasant face,
Though he would try the patience of a saint

With all his wilful ways), and calmly said,
"I wiped it out, because it was not right;
I wish it had been, for your sake, no less
Than for this pious convent's; and indeed,
The simple truth, good Padre, to confess,
I've not the least objection to succeed:
But I must please myself as well as you,
Since I must answer for the work I do."

There was St John's head, *that* I verily thought
He'd never finish. Twenty times at least
I thought it done, but still he wrought and wrought,
Defaced, remade, until at last he ceased
To work at all—went off and locked the door—
Was gone three days—then came and sat before
The picture full an hour—then calmly rose
And scratched out in a trice the mouth and nose.
This is sheer folly, as it seems to me,
Or worse than folly. Does your Highness pay
A certain sum to him for every day?
If so, the reason's very clear to see.
No? Then his brain *is* touched, assuredly.

At last, however, as you see, 'tis done—
All but our Lord's head, and the Judas there.
A month ago he finished the St John,
And has not touched it since, that I'm aware;
And now, he neither seems to think or care
About the rest, but wanders up and down
The cloistered gallery in his long dark gown,
Picking the black stones out to step upon;
Or through the garden paces listlessly
With eyes fixed on the ground, hour after hour,
While now and then he stoops and picks a flower,
And smells it, as it were, abstractedly.
What he is doing is a plague to me!
Sometimes he stands before yon orange-pot,
His hands behind him, just as if he saw
Some curious thing upon its leaves, and then,
With a quick glance, as if a sudden thought
Had struck his mind, there, standing on the spot,
He takes a little tablet out to draw,
Then, muttering to himself, walks on agen.
He is the very oddest man of men!

Brother Anselmo tells me that the book
('Twas left by chance upon the bench one day,
And in its leaves our brother got a look)
Is scribbled over with all sorts of things,—
Notes about colours, how to mix and lay,
With plans of flying figures, frames for wings,
Caricatures and forts and scaffoldings,
The skeletons of men and beasts and birds,
Engines, and cabalistic signs and words,
Some written backwards, notes of music, lyres,
And wheels with boilers under them and fires,
A sort of lute made of a horse's skull,
Sonnets, and other idle scraps of rhyme,—
Of things like this the book was scribbled full.
I pray your Highness, now, is this the way,
Instead of painting every day all day,
For him to trifle with our precious time?

Ah! there he is now—Would your Highness look
Behind that pillar in the furthest nook,
That is his velvet cap and flowing robe.

See how he pulls his beard, as up and down
He seems to count the stones he treads upon!
'Twould irk the patience of the good man Job
To see him idling thus his time away,
As if our Lord and Judas both were done,
And there was nought to do but muse and stray
Along the cloisters. May I dare to pray
Your Highness would vouchsafe one word to say;
For when I speak he only answers me,
"Padre Bandelli, go and say your mass—
That's what you understand—and let me pass;
I am not idle, though I seem to be."
"Not idle! then I'm nothing but an ass."
Thus once I spoke, for he annoyed me so;
At which he answered, smiling, "Oh no, no!
Padre, you're very wise, as all men know."
I mention this to show what pleasant ways
This painter has, and not that I the praise
Accepted as at all deserved by me.
God save us from vain pride, and help us through
Our daily work in due humility!
Not mine the praise for what I have, for *He*

Hath given all! So I began anew:
"Not idle! Well, I know not what you do!
You do not paint our picture, that I see."
To which he said, "A picture is not wrought
By hands alone, good Padre, but by thought.
In the interior life it first must start,
And grow to form and colour in the soul;
There once conceived and rounded to a whole,
The rest is but the handicraft of art.
While I seem idle, then my soul creates;
While I am painting, then my hand translates."
Now this, I say, is nonsense, sheer enough,
Or else a metaphysical excuse
For idleness, and he should not abuse
Your Highness by this sort of canting stuff.
Look at him, sauntering there in his long dress—
If he is working, what is idleness?

Not there, your Highness,—on the other side
Our painter's walking; he you look at now
Is a poor brother, pious, void of pride,
Who there performs a penitential vow.

He, like Ser Leonardo, does not stroll
Idly, but as he walks recites his prayers,
And reads his breviary; and he wears
A haircloth 'neath his serge to save his soul.
Ah! weak is man, he falls in many snares;
And we with prayer must work, would we control
Those idle thoughts where Satan sows his tares.

But, as I was observing, there have passed
Some twenty long and weary months since he
First turned us out of our refectory,
And who knows how much longer this may last?
Yet if our painter worked there steadily,
I could say nothing; but the work stands still,
While he goes idling round the cloisters' shade.
Pleasant enough for him—but is he paid
For idle dreaming thoughts, or work and skill?

I crave your pardon; if I speak amiss,
Your Highness will, I hope, allowance make
That I have spoken for your Highness' sake,
And not that us it inconveniences,

Although it is a scandal to us all
To see this picture half-done on the wall.
A word from your most gracious lips, I feel,
Would greatly quicken Ser Leonardo's zeal,
And we should soon see o'er our daily board,
The Judas finished, and our blessed Lord.

But he approaches, in his hand the book;
Into its pages should your Highness look,
They would amuse you by their strange devices.
Your gracious presence now he recognises;
That smile and bow and lifted cap I see,
Are for his Prince and Patron, not for me.

LEONARDO DA VINCI POETISES

TO

THE DUKE IN HIS OWN DEFENCE.

Padre Bandelli, then, complains of me
Because, forsooth, I have not drawn a line
Upon the Saviour's head; perhaps, then, he
Could without trouble paint that head divine.
But think, oh Signor Duca, what should be
The pure perfection of our Saviour's face—
What sorrowing majesty, what noble grace,
At that dread moment when He brake the bread,
And those submissive words of pathos said,
"By one among you I shall be betrayed,"—
And say if 'tis an easy task to find,
Even among the best that walk this earth,

The fitting type of that divinest worth,
That has its image solely in the mind.
Vainly my pencil struggles to express
The sorrowing grandeur of such holiness.
In patient thought, in ever-seeking prayer,
I strive to shape that glorious face within,
But the soul's mirror, dulled and dimmed by sin,
Reflects not yet the perfect image there.
Can the hand do before the soul has wrought?
Is not our art the servant of our thought?

And Judas, too,—the basest face I see
Will not contain his utter infamy;
Among the dregs and offal of mankind,
Vainly I seek an utter wretch to find.
He who for thirty silver coins would sell
His Lord, must be the Devil's miracle.
Padre Bandelli thinks it easy is
To find the type of him who with a kiss
Betrayed his Lord. Well, what I can I'll do;
And if it please his reverence and you,
For Judas' face I'm willing to paint his.

Padre Bandelli is a sort of man,
Joking apart, whose little round of thought
Is like his life, the measure of a span.
He knows and does the duties he is taught,—
Prays, preaches, eats, and sleeps in dull content;
Does the day's work, and deems it excellent;
Says he's a sinner, but we're sinners all,
And puts his own sin down to Adam's fall.
Christ, at the last day, others may reject,—
Poor painters, or great dukes with their state cares;
But that, with all his masses, fasts, and prayers,
A convent's prior should not be elect,
Padre Bandelli has not half a doubt—
'Twere a strange heaven, indeed, with him left out.
Him the imagination does not tease
With hungry cravings, restless impulses;
Him no despairing days the Furies bring,
No torturing doubts, no anxious questioning;
But day by day his ordered time is spent,
In doing over the same things again.
How should he know the artist's inward strain,
His vexing and fastidious discontent?

Art he considers as a sort of trade,
Like laying bricks: If one can lay a yard
In one good hour, how can it be so hard
In two good hours, that two yards should be laid?

But, Signor Duca, you can apprehend
The artist's soul—how there is ne'er an end
Of climbing fancies, longings, and desires,
That burn within him like consuming fires;
How, beaten to and fro by joy and pain,
He grasps at shadows he can ne'er retain.
How sweet and fair the inward vision gleams!
How dull and base the painted copy seems!
We are like Danaus' daughters—all in vain
We strive to fill our vases. Human art
Through myriad leaks lets out the spirit's part,
And nothing but the earthy dregs remain.

But who can force the spirit to conceive?
Its lofty empire is above our will:
Trained though we be, we only can fulfil
Its orders, and a joyous welcome give.

Oft when the music waits, the room is decked,
And hope looks out from the expectant breast,
Vainly we wait to greet the invited guest.
Oft when its presence least our souls expect,
Sudden, unsummoned, there it stands, as Eve
Stood before Adam,—as in twilight sky
The first young star—half joy, half mystery.

The wilful work built by the conscious brain
Is but the humble handicraft of art;
It has its growth in toil, its birth in pain.
The Imagination, silent and apart
Above the Will, beyond the conscious eye,
Fashions in joyous ease and as in play
Its fine creations,—mixing up alway
The real and the ideal, heaven and earth,
Darkness and sunshine; and then, pushing forth
Sudden upon our world of consciousness
Its world of wonder, leaves to us the stress,
By patient art, to copy its pure grace,
And catch the perfect features of its face.

From hand to spirit must the human chain
Be closely linked, and thence to the divine
Stretch up, through feeling, its electric line,
To draw heaven down, or all our art is vain.
For in its loftiest mood the soul obeys
A higher power that shapes our thoughts, and sways
Their motions, when by love and strong desire
We are uplifted. From a source unknown
The power descends—with its ethereal fire
Inflames us—not possessing but possessed
We do its bidding; but we do not own
The grace that in those happy hours is given,
More than its strings the music of the lyre—
More than the shower the rainbow lent by heaven.
Nature and man are only organ-keys—
Mere soundless pipes—despite our vaunted skill—
Till, with its breath, the power above us fill
The stops, and touch us to its harmonies.

Oh Signor Duca, as the woman bears
Her child, not in a moment nor a day,

So doth the soul the germ that God doth lay
Within it, with as many pains and cares.
From the whole being it absorbs and draws
Its form and life—on all we are and see
It feeds by subtle sympathetic laws;
Each sense it stirs, it fires each faculty
To hunt the outer world, and thence to seize
Food for assimilation. By degrees
Perfect it grows at last in every part,
And then is born into the world of art.

In facile natures fancies quickly grow,
But such quick fancies have but little root.
Soon the narcissus flowers and dies, but slow
The tree whose blossoms shall mature to fruit.
Grace is a moment's happy feeling, Power
A life's slow growth; and we for many an hour
Must strain and toil, and wait and weep, if we
The perfect fruit of all we are would see.

Therefore I wait. Within my earnest thought
For years upon this picture I have wrought,

Yet still it is not ripe; I dare not paint
Till all is ordered and matured within.
Hand-work and head-work have an earthly taint,
But when the soul commands I shall begin.

On themes like these I should not dare to dwell
With our good Prior—they to him would be
Mere nonsense; he must touch and taste and see;
And facts, he says, are never mystical.
Now, the fact is, our worthy Prior says,
The convent is annoyed by my delays;
Nor can he see why I for hours and days
Should muse and dream and idle here around.
I have not made a face he has not found
Quite good enough before it was half-done.
"Don't bother more," he says, "let it alone."
What can one say to such a connoisseur?
How could a Prior and a critic err?

But, not to be more tedious, I confess
I am disturbed to think I so distress

The worthy Prior. Yet 'twere wholly vain
To him an artist's feelings to explain;
But, Signor Duca, you will understand,
And so I treat on higher themes with you.
The work you order I shall strive to do
With all my soul, not merely with my hand.

RADICOFANI.

" Quivi era l'Aretin che dalle braccia
Fiere di Ghin di Tacco ebbe la morte."

I.

THIS is a barren, desolate scene,
Grim and grey, with scarce a tree,
Gashed with many a wild ravine
Far away as the eye can see;
Ne'er a home for miles to be found,
Save where huddled on some grim peak
A village clinging in fear looks round
Over the country vast and bleak,
As if it had fled from the lower ground,
Refuge from horrors there to seek.

II.

Over the spare and furzy soil
With never a waving grain-field sowed,
Raggedly winds with weary toil
The shining band of dusty road,—
Down through the river's rocky bed,
That is white and dry with summer's drought,
Or climbing some sandy hillock's head,
Over and under, in and out,
Like a struggling thing by madness led,
That wanders along in fear and doubt.

III.

What are those spots on yon sandy slope
Where the green is frayed and tattered with grey?
Are they only rocks—or sheep that crop
The meagre pasture?—one scarce can say.
This seems not a place for flowers—but behold!
How the lupine spreads its pink around,
And the clustered ginestra squanders its gold
As if it loved this barren ground;

And surely that bird is over-bold
That dares to sing o'er that grave-like mound.

IV.

It is dead and still in the middle noon ;
The sand-beds shine with a blending light,
The cicali dizzen the air with their tune,
And the sunshine seems like a curse to smite ;
The mountains around their shoulders bare
Gather a thin and shadowy veil,
And shrink from the fierce and scorching glare—
And close to the grass so withered and pale
Hovering quivers the glassy air,
And the lizards pant in their emerald mail.

V.

Think of this place in the dreary gloom
Of an autumn twilight, when the sun
Hiding in banks of clouds goes down,
And silence and shadow are coming on ;—
White mists crawl—one lurid light
Glares from the west through a broken cloud—

Rack hurries above—the dubious night
Is creeping along with its spectral crowd;
Would it, I ask, be a startling sight
To meet a ghost here than in a shroud?

VI.

One of the thousand murdered men
Who have stained the blasted soil with blood?
Does the lupine get its colour then
From some victim pashed to death in the mud?
Has the yellow ginestra the hue of the gold
From the traveller here in terror torn?
Was yon bird but a sprite, singing so bold,
That in life a maiden's form had worn,
And at night steals back in its shape of old
To haunt the darkness pale and forlorn?

VII.

Look at that castle whose ruins crown
The rocky crest of yonder height,
Still frowning over the squalid town,
That cowers beneath as if in affright.

From his eyrie there to glut his beak
The robber swooped to his shuddering prey,
And the ghosts of the past still haunt the peak
Though robber and baron have passed away.
And, hark ! was that the owl's long shriek,
Or a ghost's that flits through the ruins grey?

VIII.

'Tis blood and gold wherever I gaze,
And tangled brambles, stiff and grey,—
A scowling, ugly, terrified place,
A spot for murder and deadly fray.
On such a barren, desolate heath,
When shadows were deepening all around,
The sisters weird before Macbeth
Rising, hovered along the ground,
And echoed his inward thought of death,
And vanished again behind a mound.

IX.

Such were the thoughts that filled my breast,
Wandering here one lonely night,

When sudden behind a rock's dark crest
Uprose a shape of portentous height.
A coal-black plume from his helmet flowed,
His eyes in the vizor's shadow gleamed,
And here and there a steel-flash showed
An outline vague and dim that seemed
To hover along the dusky road
Like a thing that is neither real nor dreamed.

X.

In his hand he bore a mighty spear,
Tall as a pine and stained with blood.
Transfixed in horror and ghastly fear,
With knocking knees I before him stood.
"Who and what art thou?" I cried,
"Monstrous figure, of noiseless tread,
That out of the darkness thus dost stride?"
The black plume shook on the lofty head—
A hollow voice from the helm replied—
Hollow and vague like the voice of the dead.

XI.

"Ghino di Tacco was my name!
I come to answer your sneering thought!
Start not! Listen before you blame!
The fool condemns what he knoweth not.
Call me robber or call me knight,
But listen to me while my tale I tell.
I struck, the oppressed and weak to right:
My blows on the strong and cruel fell.
For vengeance I struck! If my hand was light
Ask Benincasa—down in hell.

XII.

" On the slopes of Arbia's banks arose
The little castle that gave me birth,
When my father's strongest, bitterest foes—
The Santafiori—cursed the earth.
Him they hated, for he was brave;
Him they hunted, for he was good.
The bandit was strong the weak to save,
The blows of his heavy sword were rude;

But treason dug for him his grave,
And the Santafiori bought his blood.

XIII.

" Ah that wild and terrible night ! "
Here the spectre his great spear raised ;
And his coal-like eyes, with angry light,
Like a furnace roused by the blast, out blazed.
" Screams of women, and groans and sighs,
Clashing of steel, a swirl of flame,
Mixed with a tumult of savage cries,
Woke me. I shouted my father's name :
When sudden, before my terrified eyes,
Through the smoke a pale shape swiftly came.

XIV.

" 'Twas my mother. She seized me in her arms,
And forth she rushed in the stormy night.
Her strained eyes glared so in wild alarm,
They scared me. I uttered a shriek of fright.
'Silence, my child, for your life !' she said.
Then swift we stole down the hillside bare,

And up again through the dark wood fled;
While the sky was lit by a lurid glare,
And the great trees, roaring overhead,
Hurtled and heaved in the bleak night air.

XV.

" To yonder castle that frowns above,
By many a devious path we went;
And nurtured there with pious love
My growing days as a boy were spent.
Night by night, when tolled for the dead
The great tower-bell, at its solemn call,
My mother, in black, with a mournful tread,
And with her a lady, dark and tall,
My childish fearful footsteps led
To a shrine built into the tower's thick wall.

XVI.

" Before a crucifix there a light
Burnt dim and sad in the gloomy shade.
And oft, in the solemn silent night,
Weeping, they kneeled with me and prayed.

One night the lady came alone.
'Where is my mother?' in fear, I cried.
Then, with a kiss and a broken tone,
'Poor child!' the lady in black replied.
And I knew by her voice my mother was gone,
And my heart grew still as it had died.

XVII.

" Years went on. My wondering heart
Strove through the shadowy veil to pierce.
I wandered many an hour apart,
And my boyish spirit grew dark and fierce.
'Whose,' I cried, 'is that heavy spear,
And that blood-stained shirt against the wall?'
'Your father's, she said.' 'Why hang they there?'
'Ask me not now—'twould your heart appal!
When you are able that spear to bear,
Vengeance is yours—you shall then know all.'

XVIII.

" 'Vengeance is yours;'—day after day
These words in secret I brooded o'er.

They cast their shade on my boyish play,
Through my dreams a painful path they wore.
I longed for manhood. Within me grew
A craving desire the key to gain
To this terrible mystery. Muscle and thew
I strove to strengthen with might and main;
For my father's spear was heavy, I knew,
And my boyish attempts to wield it vain.

XIX.

"Panting, I hacked at the mountain oak,
Till it fell with a heavy crash and groan;
The gnashing wild-boar felt my stroke—
By his heels I dragged him home alone;
Daily at tilt and sword I tried
My growing strength. I laughed at fear.
Danger to me was as a bride,
The sound of whose voice I leaped to hear.
Till at last, with a thrill of manhood's pride,
I brandished aloft my father's spear.

XX.

" Fiercely I cried, as its weight I shook,
'Read me the riddle—these arms are strong—
Longer delay I will not brook;
This heart is bold—it has waited long.'
That night I started in wild surprise;
For a voice cried out, in my dreaming ear,
'Son of a murdered man, arise!
The hour is come!' 'Behold me here!'
I answered;—and there, before my eyes,
Was the form of the lady standing near.

XXI.

" Sternly she took me by the hand,
And straight to the chapel my steps she led.
I saw the spear by the altar stand;
The bloody shirt was across it spread.
The open Evangel before me stood.
'There,' as she grasped my arm, she cried,
'Are the last red drops of your father's blood,
When under the headsman's axe he died.

For know that he fell not in battle feud,
As a soldier falls, at his comrade's side.

XXII.

" ' Vainly he fought in that fearful fray
When his castle was stormed; but a faithful few
Bore him, senseless and wounded, away,—
And a bandit's life thenceforth he knew.
From lair to lair, o'er the mountains steep,
Like a wounded lion, they tracked his way.
His sword drank blood;—but in his sleep
The Santafiori seized their prey.
They dared not kill; but their plot was deep,—
And a base judge gave him to death for pay.

XXIII.

" ' Ere on the scaffold fell his head,
He called a vassal, and said, "This spear,
And the shirt my murdered blood makes red,
Are the heritage of Ghino dear.
When he can bear and wield it well,
Tell him the tale of his father's death;

How he shall use it his heart will tell.
I bless him now with my latest breath.
Say to his mother——" His voice here fell—
Your mother is sleeping this stone beneath.

XXIV.

" 'Struck, as by death, when she heard his fate
She fell, for her strength with her hope had fled.
On her grave you stand. I, forced to wait,
Tell you for her the words of the dead.
See! the Evangel is under your hand!
Swear to revenge your father's fame!
Burn on your heart, as with a brand,
Benincasa's accursed name!
Seek him in Rome—where the plot was planned
That doomed your father to death and shame!

XXV.

" 'Bind that bloody shirt to your heart!
Lift the spear! The bell strikes one—
The gates are open—at once depart,
And never return till your duty 's done.

This is no longer a home for you—
You look like your father standing there,—
If in your veins his blood runs true
You know what there is to do and dare.
Go! if this story thrill you through,
Swear to revenge your father. Swear!

XXVI.

"'Go! When that villain's head you bring,
Bridge shall fall, and portcullis rise,
And the bells of Radicofani ring;
But never till then dare meet these eyes.'
The light burned dim as thus she spoke;
I grasped the spear with a thrill of rage;
I struck my clenched hand on the book
And swore my oath on the holy page,
Never again on the place to look
Till his blood my vengeance should assuage.

XXVII.

"The grinding bridge with a clang went down,
The tempest roared—the lightning flashed—

The wind through the great gate sucked such a groan
As my horse's hoofs on its pavement dashed.
Four hundred horsemen were at my side—
One word, and their swift swords left the sheath,
And crossed with a clash. Vengeance! they cried—
To Rome! Then over the sandy heath
Closely we galloped, a long fierce ride
To Rome, with the settled purpose of death.

XXVIII.

"Alone at the Campidoglio's base
I stood. The hated shape was there;
The Senator's foul and ugly face,
That brought my father to his despair;
The cursed, livid, hideous head,
With flabby mouth, and streamy eyes—
He heard in the hall my armèd tread.
He looked with a leer of cold surprise,
And 'What do you seek of me?' he said.
'A debt!' I answered, 'a bloody prize!'

XXIX.

"He started and trembled in ghastly fright,
For a terrible memory on him smote,—
My father I seemed to his bleary sight.
'Villain,' I said, as I grasped his throat,
'Go down to hell in your despair!'
A strangled gasp from his lips there came,
'Save me! oh God!'—'Go! Judas, bear
To God your deeds of crime and shame!
Turrino di Tacco is waiting there!
The mercy you meted to him—reclaim!'

XXX.

"I plunged my dagger into his heart,—
His head from his bleeding trunk I hewed,—
His vassals terrified stood apart
As I strode through the gathering multitude,—
I stuck that head on my father's spear.
'Room!' I cried, as my sword I drew;
'He meets the fate of this villain here
Who hinders my path!' They saw and knew

Death in my eyes. They left me clear
My path, and I strode in safety through.

XXXI.

"Swift to the castle's bridge I sped.
'Down with the drawbridge, men of mine!'
High up I lifted the ghastly head.
'Down with the bridge! You know the sign.'
Clang went the chains with a clattering din.
The castle's lady I found in prayer
At the lonely shrine as I entered in.
She lifted her eyes. 'You, Ghino! where
Is the traitor's head?' 'He died in his sin;'
And I flung the head on the pavement there.

XXXII.

"Then through Siena rose a cry,
But the Santafiori strove in vain;
From the eyrie of Radicofani
I swooped and swept them from hill and plain.
Their castles I burned, their lands laid waste,

Refuge they sought in the city's wall,
The cup they had proffered was theirs to taste;
I saw my foes before me fall,
But a price on my bandit head was placed.

XXXIII.

"Yet never, a bandit though I was,
Was my sword disgraced by useless crime;
With the weak and poor I made my cause,
And my deeds were sung in many a rhyme.
At my table the beggar found a feast,
Though the cruel baron felt my sword;
I sheared the ambitious worldly priest,
But the ruined peasant his farm restored;
Cursed by the proud—by the humble blessed—
I broke no promise in act or word.

XXXIV.

"There rots my castle on yonder height!—
Mortal! this promise of you I claim,
Tell the story I tell to-night
Whenever you mention Di Tacco's name."

"I promise," I cried. The figure bowed
His lofty stature and clinched his spear,
And slow, like the mist of a fading cloud,
In the shadow I watched it disappear.
And my heart in my bosom beat aloud
With a feeling of mystery, doubt, and fear.

IN THE ANTECHAMBER

OF

MONSIGNORE DEL FIOCCO.

Our master will be Cardinal ere long—
Is he not made for one?—so smooth and plump,
With those broad jaws, those half-shut peeping eyes,
Those ankle-heavy legs and knotty feet,
Which only need red stockings. Even now
He totters round with the true Cardinal's gait
Upon his tender toes, while you behind
Demurely follow, scarce an ear-shot off,
The pious footsteps of the holy man.
How many years have you thus stalked along
Behind that broad-brimmed, purple-tasselled hat,

In your stiff lace and livery, trained to pause
Whene'er he pauses, turning half to fix
His *Fifthly* on his fingers to some dull
Cringing Abbate shuffling at his side?
Then, when that point is drilled into his brain
(Proving the blessedness of poverty,
Or how the devil has no cursed wiles
To lure the world to hell like liberty—
The only one great good being obedience),
Back go the hands beneath the creased black silk
That streams behind, and on you march again;
While the gilt carriage lumbers in the rear,
And the black stallions nod their tufted crests.

Yours is a noble station, clinging there
Behind it as you clatter through the town,
Your white calves shaking with the pavement's jar,
The mark and sneer of half the world you meet.
Ah, well! 'tis wretched business yours and mine;
I know not which is worst—but then it pays;
The cards are dirty, but what matters dirt
To those who win? Though now the stakes are small,

We'll hold the court-cards when the suit is red;—
And so it will be soon; why, even now
I seem to see red stockings on his legs;—
And yesterday I said, "Your Eminence,"
As if I thought he now was Cardinal—
"Your Eminence," indeed! At that he smiled
That oily smile of his, and rubbed his hands—
Those thick fat hands, on which his emerald ring
Flashes ('tis worth at least a thousand crowns)—
And said, "Good Giacomo, not 'Eminence,'
I'm but a Monsignor, and that's too much
For my deserts." Then I, "Your 'Reverence'
Ought to be 'Eminence,' and will be soon;
The tassel's almost old upon your hat."
"*Sei matto, Giacomo,*" he said, and smiled.
You know those smiles, that glitter falsely o'er
His smooth broad cheeks, as if he asked of you,
"Am I not kind and good?" and all the while
Your soul protests, and calls out "Knave and cheat."
But, then, how can one call him by such names,
When, even with that smile upon his face,
He slips a scudo in one's hand and says,

"Go, Giacomo, and drink my health with this"?
What can one do but bow and try to blush?
"Oh—Eminenza—thanks—you are too good."

Dear man! sweet man! in all those troublous times
What zeal was his!—how earnestly he worked!
Who can forget his pure self-sacrifice,
His virtuous deeds, above this world's reward—
Done for pure Christian duty—done, of course,
For Holy Church—all was for Holy Church—
(Without a notion of this world's reward)—
All for the good of souls and Holy Church—
(*Ora pro nobis*, and that sort of thing)—
All to bring sinners back again to God,
And from the harvest root the devil's tares—
In omnia sæcula—amen—amen.
We don't forget—well! you know whom I mean
No need to mention names, though no one's nigh;
We don't forget him whose anointed hands
Were flayed by order of his Reverence,
Ere with his bleeding palms they led him down
Into the court-yard, and we, peeping through

The half-closed blind, saw him throw up his hands
And forward fall upon his face, and writhe,
When the sharp volley rang against the walls.

Those oily fingers wrote that sentence down!
That thick voice, with a hypocritic tone,
While both his palms were raised, decreed that doom.
Who could help weeping when that pious man,
Professing horror at his victim's crime,
And bidding him confess and pray to God,
And saying, "God would pardon him, perhaps,
As he himself would, if the power were his,
But, being the instrument of Church and State,
No choice was given," with his priestly foot
Pushed, you know whom, into a felon's grave?
That bloody stain is still upon the walls,
Of the same colour as the scarlet hat
Our master soon will wear; and, after all,
Who more deserves it? If he stained his soul,
Is not the labourer worthy of his hire?
He shall be raised who doth abase himself!
The good and faithful servant shall be made

The ruler over many! Ah! my friend,
He nothing lost by all those deeds of his.
He erred in zeal, but zeal is not a vice—
'Twas all for Holy Church. His secret life,
Perhaps, was not quite perfect! Who of you
Is without sin let him first cast a stone;—
No one, you see; so let us think no more
Of that. Does any Duchess smile the less
At all his compliments and unctuous words
As, leaning o'er her chair, his downcast eyes
He fixes somewhat lower than her lips,—
Upon the jewels on her neck, perchance,
He is so modest,—and with undertone
Whispers, and, deprecating, lifts his hands,
While with her fan she covers half her face?
He knows as well as any man that lives
How far to venture;—covers his foul jokes
With honeyed words, so ladies swallow them;—
Treads on the edge of scandal—not a chance
He will fall in; knows all the secret shoals
Of innuendo;—in pure earnestness
(Oh, nothing more) he seizes their soft hands

And holds them—presses them, as to enforce
His argument;—for this, our Monsignor,
Lifted above temptation, with, of course,
No carnal thought, may do before the world—
Because it must be done through innocence.
Fie on his foul mouth who should hint 'twas wrong!
Who'd be more shock'd than he, the pious man?
He would go home and pray for that lost soul!

And yet, how can a woman pure in heart,
Without disgust, accept his compliments,
And let him feed on her his gloating eyes?
Of course, it's just because she's innocent.
Yes! I am lean and dry, a servitor,
Not fat and oily like our Monsignor,
And so I can't endure his nauseous ways;—
All right, of course! But yet I sometimes think,
Did San Pietro talk to Martha thus,
And every night, wearing his fisherman's ring,
Show his silk-stocking'd legs in soft saloons,
And fish for women with a net like this?

Those soft fat hands—those sweet anointed hands—
Those hands that wear the glittering emerald ring—
Those hands whose palms are pressed so oft in prayer—
Those hands that fondle high-born ladies' hands—
Those hands that give their blessing to the poor—
Those hateful, hideous hands are red with blood!
Think! Principessa, when you kiss those hands—
Think! Novice, when those hands upon your head
Are laid in consecration—think of this!

Stop, Master Giacomo! don't get too warm!
When Monsignore gave you yesterday,
With those same hateful, hideous, bloody hands,
Your scudo, did you take it, sir, or not?
Yes! I confess! the world will be the world!
One must not ask too much of mortal man,
Nor mortal woman neither, Giacomo!
But yet we cannot always keep a curb
Upon our feelings, school them as we will;
And I, who bow and cringe and smile all day,
Detest at times my very self, and grow
So restive 'neath my rank hypocrisy,

I must break loose and fling out like a horse
In useless kicks, or else I should go mad.
God knows I hate this man, and so at times,
Rather than take him by the throat, I come
And pour my passion out in idle words;
They ease me. You're my friend; but if I thought
A word of this would reach his ears; but, no!
We know each other both too well for that.

One or two questions I should like to ask,
If Monsignor would only answer them,
As this—what Sora Lisa says to him
At her confession, once a-week at least
(For Monsignor, having her soul in charge,
When she don't come to him, must go to her).
She used to be so poor, but times are changed,
And Sora Lisa keeps her carriage now;
And those old gowns, by some "Hey, presto, change,"
Have turned to rustling silks; and at her ears
Diamonds and rubies dangle, which she shows,
When she's the mind, in her own opera box.
Well! well! that office our good Monsignor

Gave her poor husband from pure love of him
May pay for these; and if it don't, why, then,
It don't—what business is it of ours?
And then, who knows, some uncle may have died
(Uncles are always dying for such folks)
And made her rich;—why should we peep and pry?
Her soul is safe at least with Monsignor.

And this reminds me—did you ever know
Nina, that tall, majestic, fierce-eyed girl,
With blue-black hair, which, when she loosed it, shook
Its crimpled darkness almost to the floor?—
She that was friend to Monsignor while yet
He was a humble Abbé—born indeed
In the same town and came to live in Rome?
Not know her? She, I mean, who disappeared
Some ten years back, and God knows how or why?
Well, Nina,—are you sure there's no one near?—
Nina—

Per Dio! how his stinging bell
Startled my blood, as if the Monsignor
Cried out, "You, Giacomo; what, there again

At your old trick of talking? Hold your tongue!"
And so I will, per Bacco, so I will;—
Who tells no secrets breaks no confidence.
Nature, as Monsignor has often said,
Gave us two eyes, two ears, and but one tongue,
As if to say, "Tell half you see and hear;"
And I'm an ass to let my tongue run on,
After such lessons. There he rings again!
Vengo—per Dio—Vengo subito.

A CONTEMPORARY CRITICISM:

IN WHICH FEDERIGO DI MONTAFELTRO, DUKE OF URBINO, GIVES HIS VIEWS OF RAFFAELLE.

[*Dedicated to H. G. W.*]

OH! I admit his talent,—there's no lack
Of facile talent; what in him I blame
Is that he travels in his master's track
With such a slavish, imitative aim.
'Tis Perugino all, from head to foot:
Angels the same, with their affected grace,
Playing the lyre with sideway upturned face;
Round-faced, small-eyed Madonnas,—all the same.
Landscapes mere copies; subjects, branch and root,
His master's subjects,—not an arch or shaft

Of all his architecture, but you see
That too is copied. Every little shoot
Upon his genius is his master's graft.
And yet, through all, there's clear ability.
Why will he never grow his special fruit?

Lately he's striven to effect a change,
But still an imitator he must go,
From peaceful Perugino's timid range
To the extravagance of Angelo,
Behind them both, of course, in both their ways;
For, as uncompromising Michael says,
"Who follows after, cannot go before."

Then why, too, will he try so many things?
Instead of sticking to one single art,
He must be studying music, twanging strings,
And writing sonnets, with their "heart and dart."
Lately, he's setting up for architect,
And planning palaces; and, as I learn,
Has made a statue,—every art in turn,—
Like Leonardo (and you recollect,

How with his many arts even he was wrecked);
But if *he* failed, what can this youth expect?

A touch of this same vice his father had:
He laid aside the brush to use the pen;
And though he praised my deeds,—and I, of men,
Should be the last to call the praising bad,
Though over-praised,—yet, be the truth confest,
No man in more than one art can be best.

'Twas but the other day I spoke to him,
With earnest hope to make him change his course;
I told him he would dissipate his force
By following the lead of every whim,
And (for I like the youth, and recognise
In all his efforts good abilities)
I urged upon him not to skip and skim
In many arts, but give himself to one,
For life was quite too short for everything,
And doing all things, nothing gets well done.

He thanked me for my kindness, disagreed

With my conclusions in a modest way
(He's modest, *that* 'tis only just to say);
But in a letter that he sends to-day
Here is his answer. Listen, while I read.

"Most noble sir,"—and so on, and so on,—
"A thousand thanks," — hem — hem, — "in one so high,"
"Learned in art,"—et cetera,—"I shall try"—
Oh! that's about his picture,—"critic's eye;"
"Patron,"—pho, pho—where *has* the passage gone?
Ah! here we come to it at last:—"You thought,"
He says, "that in too many arts I wrought;
And you advised me to stick close to one.
Thanks for your gracious counsel, all too kind;
And answering, if I chance to speak my mind
Too boldly, pardon. Yet it seems to me
All arts are one—all branches on one tree,—
All fingers, as it were, upon one hand.
You ask me to be thumb alone; but pray,
Reft of the answering fingers Nature planned,
Is not the hand deformed for work or play?

"Or rather take, to illustrate my thought,
Music, the only art to science wrought,
The ideal art, that underlies the whole,
Interprets all, and is of all the soul.
Each art is, so to speak, a separate tone;
The perfect chord results from all in one.
Strike one, and as its last vibrations die,
Listen,—from all the other tones a cry
Wails forth, half-longing and half-prophecy.
So does the complement, the hint, the germ
Of every art within the others lie,
And in their inner essence all unite;
For what is melody but fluid form,
Or form, but fixed and stationed melody?
Colours are but the silent chords of light,
Touched by the painter into tone and key,
And harmonised in every changeful hue.
So colours live in sound,—the trumpet blows
Its scarlet, and the flute its tender blue;
The perfect statue, in its pale repose,
Has for the soul a melody divine,
That lingers dreaming round each subtle line,

And stills the gazer lest its charm he lose.
So rhythmic words, strung by the poet, own
Music and form and colour—every sense
Rhymes with the rest;—'tis in the means alone
The various arts receive their difference."

Vague, idle talk! such stuff as this I call;
Pretty for girls—quite metaphysical,
Almost poetic, if you will; but then,
For you and me, or any reasoning men,
All visionary, vague, impractical.
Such silly jargon lacks all common sense;
How can he dream it helps him paint, to know
The way to tinkle on ten instruments?
Or does he fancy writing rhymes assists
In laying colours? Bah! he's in the mists.

But let's go on. Here's something, I admit,
That shows a less deficiency of wit.

"Life is too short perfection to attain,
We all are maimed; and do the best we can,

Each trade deforms us with the overstrain
Of some too favoured faculty or sense,
O'er-fostered at the others' vast expense.
Yet why should one Art be the others' bane?
The perfect artist should be perfect man.
Oh! let at least our theory be grand,
To make a whole man, not to train a hand;
Rearing our temple, let it be our pride
Nought to neglect, but build with patient care
A perfect temple, finished everywhere,
And not a mere façade with one good side."

Of course, of course, if we were gods; but then,
Life is so short, and we are only men.
These youths, these youths — there's really something great
In their ambitions. Let our friend but wait,
And Time will snuff his dreams out, one by one.
I had such dreams once. How they all have gone!

"If I the model of a man should seek,
Where should I find him? Though the blacksmith's arm

Is muscled well, his lower limbs are weak,
His shoulders curved. The student shall I take?
His o'erworked brain has cost his body harm.
No; he alone will serve who equal strain
Has given each, the body and the brain;
One who, like you, most gracious Duke, has known
The whole man into consonance to train.
Grace from consent of every force is shown,
Not where one's loss has been another's gain."

Well put, my Raffaelle; it will never do
To such an argument to say, "not true."

"Besides, the varied tasking of the mind
Not only makes us sane, but keeps us strong.
The noblest faculty when strained too long
Turns to convention,—wearied, seeks to find
In repetition solace and repose.
'Tis only the fresh arm that strikes great blows.
Fallow and change we need, not constant toil,
Not always the same crop on the same soil.
To stretch our powers demands an earnest strain,

And rest, to strengthen what by work we gain.
Sleeping, the body grows in thews and brain."

That's true, at least—the body must have sleep!
I'm glad to find one statement here at last
With which I can most cordially agree.
Shall I read more, or is your patience past?
Oh!—as to his originality,
Here are a few words taken from a heap.
One moment first,—here's something not to skip.

"But please remember, of the famous names,
Who is there hath confined him to one art,
Giotto, Da Vinci, or Orcagna? No,—
Or our great living master, Angelo,—
They are whole men, whose rounded knowledge shames
  Our narrow study of a single part;
  Not merely painters, dwarfed in all their aims,
  But men who painted, builded, carved, and wrote:
  Whole diapasons—not a separate note."

  Now for that other passage,—let us see
  His thoughts about originality.

"In one sense no man is original,—
Borrowers and beggars are we, one and all.
Art, science, thought, grow up from age to age,
And all are palimpsests upon Time's page.
Our loftiest pedestals are tombs;—the seed
Sown by the dead and living in us grow;
And what we are is tinged by what we know.
As from the air our sustenance we draw,
So from all thought our private thought we feed,
Germs strewn from other minds within us breed,
And no one is his own unaided law.
Nor from the age alone we take our hue,
But by the narrower mould of accident
A form and colour to our life is lent;
As under blue sky grows the water blue,
Or clouds unto the mountain's shape are bent.

"Yet each man, following his sympathies,
Unto himself assimilating all,
Using men's thoughts and forms as steps to rise,
Who speaks at last his individual word,
The free result of all things seen and heard,

Is in the noblest sense original.
Each to himself must be his final rule,
Supreme dictator, to reject or use,
Employing what he takes but as his tool.
But he who, self-sufficient, dares refuse
All aid of men, must be a god or fool.

"I took Lippino's figure for St Paul:
What then? I made it, in the taking, mine,
And gave it new life in a new design.
I worked in Perugino's style, but all
My own my pictures were in every line.
By sympathy of feeling and of thought,
Not coldly copying, in his forms I wrought.
The theme of the Entombment, I admit,
Was from an old sarcophagus of stone;
But to another purpose using it,
Its new expression made it all my own.
From all great men and minds I freely learn,
Orcagna, Giotto, Michael, each in turn,
Thank them for help, and taking what I find,
Stamp on their forms the pressure of my mind.

Well! who that ever lived did not the same?
Name me of all the great names but one name—
Old Homer? Phidias? Virgil?—and more low
In time, not power, Da Vinci? Angelo?
'Tis the small nature dares not to receive,
Having no wealth within from which to give.
The greatest minds the greatest debts may owe,
And by their taking make a thing to live.

"Did our Da Vinci scorn, with studious zeal,
Massaccio's nature, Lippi's strength to steal?
Is Giotto's campanile, soaring there
Like music up into our Florence air,
Unfathered by an ancestry of towers?
Or is the round of great St Peter's dome,
That Michael now is swinging over Rome,
Without a debt to this grand dome of ours?
And Brunelleschi, did he never see
The globed Pantheon's massive dignity?
These men are copyists, then! But, after all,
If these are not, who is original?

"Look round upon our Florence—each to each
See! how her earnest minds and hearts unite,
And buttressed thus in strength attain a height
Which none could ever hope alone to reach!
Or, like a serried phalanx all inspired
By one great hope, and moving to one end,
How strength and daring each to each they lend,
As on they press, undaunted and untired!
Each fighting for the truth, and one for all,
With no mean pride to be original."

Well! here the true and false are mixed with skill;
But let him talk and reason as he will,
I'm of the same opinion as before;—
A man must strive to be original,
And give himself to one art, not to all.
Besides, the names and facts he numbers o'er
Prove but the rule, being exceptions still.
But, after all, the subject is a bore;
And, Signor Sanzio, you and all your talk
(Which, I'll confess, is not entirely ill)
Have our permission to withdraw.

Pray walk
Upon the balcony. Is any sight
More fair than Florence in this hazy light,
Sleeping all silent in the afternoon,
Like the enchanted beauty, full of rest,
Her bride-like veil spread careless on her breast?
Our June this year has been a peerless June.

ANTIQUE

K

CLEOPATRA.

[*Dedicated to J. L. M.*]

HERE, Charmian, take my bracelets,
  They bar with a purple stain
My arms; turn over my pillows—
  They are hot where I have lain:
Open the lattice wider,
  A gauze o'er my bosom throw,
And let me inhale the odours
  That over the garden blow.

I dreamed I was with my Antony,
  And in his arms I lay;
Ah, me! the vision has vanished—
  The music has died away.

The flame and the perfume have perished—
  As this spiced aromatic pastille
That wound the blue smoke of its odour
  Is now but an ashy hill.

Scatter upon me rose-leaves,
  They cool me after my sleep,
And with sandal odours fan me
  Till into my veins they creep;
Reach down the lute, and play me
  A melancholy tune,
To rhyme with the dream that has vanished,
  And the slumbering afternoon.

There, drowsing in golden sunlight,
  Loiters the slow smooth Nile,
Through slender papyri, that cover
  The wary crocodile.
The lotus lolls on the water,
  And opens its heart of gold,
And over its broad leaf-pavement
  Never a ripple is rolled.

The twilight breeze is too lazy
  Those feathery palms to wave,
And yon little cloud is as motionless
  As a stone above a grave.

Ah, me! this lifeless nature
  Oppresses my heart and brain!
Oh! for a storm and thunder—
  For lightning and wild fierce rain!
Fling down that lute—I hate it!
  Take rather his buckler and sword,
And crash them and clash them together
  Till this sleeping world is stirred.

Hark! to my Indian beauty—
  My cockatoo, creamy white,
With roses under his feathers—
  That flashes across the light.
Look! listen! as backward and forward
  To his hoop of gold he clings,
How he trembles, with crest uplifted,
  And shrieks as he madly swings!

Oh, cockatoo, shriek for Antony!
  Cry, "Come, my love, come home!"
Shriek, "Antony! Antony! Antony!"
  Till he hears you even in Rome.

There—leave me, and take from my chamber
  That stupid little gazelle,
With its bright black eyes so meaningless,
  And its silly tinkling bell!
Take him,—my nerves he vexes—
  The thing without blood or brain,—
Or, by the body of Isis,
  I'll snap his thin neck in twain!

Leave me to gaze at the landscape
  Mistily stretching away,
Where the afternoon's opaline tremors
  O'er the mountains quivering play;
Till the fiercer splendour of sunset
  Pours from the west its fire,
And melted, as in a crucible,
  Their earthy forms expire;

And the bald blear skull of the desert
  With glowing mountains is crowned,
That burning like molten jewels
  Circle its temples round.

I will lie and dream of the past time,
  Æons of thought away,
And through the jungle of memory
  Loosen my fancy to play;
When, a smooth and velvety tiger,
  Ribbed with yellow and black,
Supple and cushion-footed
  I wandered, where never the track
Of a human creature had rustled
  The silence of mighty woods,
And, fierce in a tyrannous freedom,
  I knew but the law of my moods.
The elephant, trumpeting, started,
  When he heard my footstep near,
And the spotted giraffes fled wildly
  In a yellow cloud of fear.

I sucked in the noontide splendour,
 Quivering along the glade,
Or yawning, panting, and dreaming,
 Basked in the tamarisk shade,
Till I heard my wild mate roaring,
 As the shadows of night came on,
To brood in the trees' thick branches
 And the shadow of sleep was gone;
Then I roused, and roared in answer,
 And unsheathed from my cushioned feet
My curving claws, and stretched me,
 And wandered my mate to greet.
We toyed in the amber moonlight,
 Upon the warm flat sand,
And struck at each other our massive arms—
 How powerful he was and grand!
His yellow eyes flashed fiercely
 As he crouched and gazed at me,
And his quivering tail, like a serpent,
 Twitched curving nervously.
Then like a storm he seized me,
 With a wild triumphant cry,

And we met, as two clouds in heaven
  When the thunders before them fly.
We grappled and struggled together,
  For his love like his rage was rude;
And his teeth in the swelling folds of my neck
  At times, in our play, drew blood.

Often another suitor—
  For I was flexile and fair—
Fought for me in the moonlight,
  While I lay couching there,
Till his blood was drained by the desert;
  And, ruffled with triumph and power,
He licked me and lay beside me
  To breathe him a vast half-hour.
Then down to the fountain we loitered,
  Where the antelopes came to drink;
Like a bolt we sprang upon them,
  Ere they had time to shrink.
We drank their blood and crushed them,
  And tore them limb from limb,

And the hungriest lion doubted
  Ere he disputed with him.

That was a life to live for!
  Not this weak human life,
With its frivolous bloodless passions,
  Its poor and petty strife!

Come to my arms, my hero,
  The shadows of twilight grow,
And the tiger's ancient fierceness
  In my veins begins to flow.
Come not cringing to sue me!
  Take me with triumph and power,
As a warrior storms a fortress!
  I will not shrink or cower.
Come, as you came in the desert,
  Ere we were women and men,
When the tiger passions were in us,
  And love as you loved me then!

CASSANDRA.*

[*Dedicated to H. C.*]

WHY didst thou lift the veil, beloved one,
Divine Apollo, from these human eyes?
The phantom forms that from the Future rise
Appal me; all in vain I seek to shun
This fatal knowledge; horror-struck to see
The shadowy shapes of coming destiny
Steal forth unsummoned fierce with death and hate,
But powerless to avert the doom of Fate.
Ah! better blindness, better night, dark night!

* A chronological licence has been taken in this poem, which it is hoped will be pardoned in view of the mythical character of the period.

Better dead loss of that supreme delight,
Thy love! better the worst that Time conceals
Than all the coming horrors it reveals.
Shroud me again in darkness—close the door
Of the dread Future—torture me no more.
With these foul shapes of visionary crime—
These murders that stare through the veil of time,—
These horrors—drive these fearful sights away,
Or give me power the coming crime to stay.
Only in ignorance is joy; to rest
In blind fond trust upon the Present's breast.
'Tis more than death, far more, to see, to know;
Take back the gift! We creatures here below
Need all our blindness, need the mortal veil
Which shuts the Future out, obscures the sense,
And hides us from our Fate. Not too much light
May man endure. Pure truth is too intense,
It blinds us. Perfect Love at its full height
Kills with excess of rapture. We are made
With human senses, and we all need here
Illusions, veils, a tempering atmosphere,
And ignorance to shield us with its shade—

Ye Gods in heaven may see and know, not fear
The face of Fate, serene, beyond all care;
But when to us poor mortals you appear,
Around your glory ye a veil must wear,
Or who could look and live? And so to me
Divinest of the Gods you came; too bright
For all your mortal veil, suffused with light,
Radiant with splendours of divinity.

Ah! what a price for Love I paid! no more,
Since that dread gift, the peace, the tranquil bliss
That once in my unburdened heart I bore!
No more the careless, thoughtless happiness,
The maiden hope, the unreasoning faith, the scent
Of vague sweet feelings making redolent
The inmost chambers of my life; 'tis o'er—
Fled—vanished. The soft veil is rent away.
Where'er I set my feet on the soft grass
'Tis stained with blood. The glory of the day
Is darkened with foul crimes. The shapes that pass
Before my scared and visionary eyes
No more are gentle dreams, but ghosts that rise

And mock and threaten from the unopened tomb
Of the black Future, and with voice of doom,
Faint, dim, but horrible, dismay my soul.

Hark ! as I speak—those voices—that fierce jar—
That murmurous tumult hurrying from afar—
What means it ? Close my eyes, my ears control !
They come, still nearer, up the sounding stair.
What horror now is brooding o'er this place ?
What dreadful crime ? What does Medea there
In that dim chamber ? See on her dark face
And serpent brow, rage, fury, love, despair !
What seeks she ? There her children are at play
Laughing and talking. Not so fierce, I say,
You scare them with that passionate embrace !
Hark to those footsteps in the hall—the loud
Clear voice of Jason heard above the crowd.
Why does she push them now so stern away
And listening glance around,—then fixed and mute,
Her brow shut down, her mouth irresolute,
Her thin hands twitching at her robes the while,
As with some fearful purpose does she stand ?

Why that triumphant glance—that hideous smile—
That poniard hidden in her mantle there,
That through the dropping folds now darts its gleam?
Oh Gods! oh, all ye Gods! hold back her hand.
Spare them! oh, spare them! oh, Medea, spare!
You will not, dare not! ah, that sharp shrill scream!
Ah!—the red blood—'tis trickling down the floor!
Help! help! oh, hide me! Let me see no more!

PAN IN LOVE.

Stop running more. You must—indeed you shall.
See how your feet are hurt. Your breath comes fast
And all in vain. Light as you are, you see
I can outrun you, and these briers and brakes
That tear your tender feet will never harm
My horny hoofs. Why do you fly from me?
I mean no ill. Stop. Rest upon this bank,
Soft with green mosses, sprinkled with quaint flowers,
And listen to me while you get your breath.
Bacchus is in the distant vale, so far
His cymbals scarcely reach us—far away
Silenus and his rout—they'll never hear
Though you should scream with all your little voice.

I am a coarse, rough fellow, but I love
Such smooth, white-limbed, soft-footed things as you.
What shall I do to make you love me back,
And twine those arms around this hairy neck?
What shall I give you for a kiss? Come, sit
On these rough shaggy knees, and smooth my cheeks
With your soft hands. Bacchus is fairer far;
But he, the fickle, vain, conceited god,
Loves but himself, and changes every hour
For some new fancy. I will be more true,
And love for ever. Ah! we ugly gods
Alone are constant, and that Venus knew
When she preferred to all the dandy crew
Stern, black, old Vulcan.

Oh! dear little feet!
Dear little hands, so rosy, tapering, slight.
See, how they look against these hands and hoofs,
That never will be tired to work for you.

Nay! if you will not sit upon my knee,
Lie on that bank, and listen while I play

A sylvan song upon these reedy pipes.
In the full moonrise as I lay last night
Under the alders on Peneus' banks,
Dabbling my hoofs in the cool stream, that welled
Wine-dark with gleamy ripples round their roots,
I made the song the while I shaped the pipes.
'Tis all of you and love, as you shall hear.
The drooping lilies, as I sang it, heaved
Upon their broad green leaves, and underneath,
Swift silvery fishes, poised on quivering fins,
Hung motionless to listen; in the grass
The crickets ceased to shrill their tiny bells;
And even the nightingale, that all the eve
Hid in the grove's deep green, had throbbed and thrilled,
Paused in his strain of love to list to mine.
Bacchus is handsome, but such songs as this
He cannot shape, and better loves the clash
Of brazen cymbals than my reedy pipes.
Fair as he is without, he's coarse within—
Gross in his nature, loving noise and wine;
And, tipsy, half the time goes reeling round,
Leaning on old Silenus' shoulders fat.

But I have scores of songs that no one knows,
Not even Apollo, no, nor Mercury—
Their strings can never sing like my sweet pipes—
Some, that will make fierce tigers rub their fur
Against the oak-trunks for delight, or stretch
Their plump sides for my pillow on the sward.
Some, that will make the satyrs' clattering hoofs
Leap when they hear, and from their noonday dreams
Start up to stamp a wild and frolic dance
In the green shadows. Ay! and better songs,
Made for the delicate nice ears of nymphs,
Which while I sing my pipes shall imitate
The droning bass of honey-seeking bees,
The tinkling tenor of clear pebbly streams,
The breezy alto of the alder's sighs,
And all the airy sounds that lull the grove
When noon falls fast asleep among the hills.
Nor only these,—for I can pipe to you
Songs that will make the slippery vipers pause,
And stay the stags to gaze with their great eyes;
Such songs—and you shall hear them, if you will—
That Bacchus' self would give his hide to hear.

If you'll but love me every day I'll bring
The coyest flowers, such as you never saw,
To deck you with. I know their secret nooks—
They cannot hide themselves away from Pan.
And you shall have rare garlands; and your bed
Of fragrant mosses shall be sprinkled o'er
With violets like your eyes—just for a kiss.
Love me, and you shall do whate'er you like,
And shall be tended wheresoe'er you go,
And not a beast shall hurt you—not a toad
But at your bidding give his jewel up.
The speckled shining snakes shall never sting,
But twist like bracelets round your rosy arms,
And keep your bosom cool in the hot noon.
You shall have berries ripe of every kind,
And luscious peaches, and wild nectarines,
And sunflecked apricots, and honeyed dates,
And wine from bee-stung grapes drunk with the sun
(Such wine as Bacchus never tasted yet).
And not a poisonous plant shall have the power
To tetter your white flesh if you'll love Pan.

And then I'll tell you tales that no one knows;
Of what the pines talk in the summer nights
When far above you hear them murmuring
As they sway whispering to the lifting breeze—
And what the storm shrieks to the struggling oaks
As it flies through them hurrying to the sea
From mountain crags and cliffs. Or, when you're sad,
I'll tell you tales that solemn cypresses
Have whispered to me. There's not anything
Hid in the woods and dales and dark ravines,
Shadowed in dripping caves, or by the shore,
Slipping from sight, but I can tell to you.
Plump, dull-eared Bacchus, thinking of himself,
Never can catch a syllable of this;
But with my shaggy ear against the grass
I hear the secrets hidden underground,
And know how in the inner forge of Earth,
The pulse-like hammers of creation beat.
Old Pan is ugly, rough, and rude to see,
But no one knows such secrets as old Pan.
What shall I give you for a kiss? I must,

Will have it. See, these iris-coloured shells,
So curiously veined with gleamy pearl—
Rare shells, that Venus covets, and would give
A thousand kisses for—shall all be yours ;—
And these great pearls too, and red coral beads,
Worn round by the smooth sea,—you shall have all.
Strung on your neck, and, rolling there between
Your budding breasts, how pretty they will look !
Do not refuse old Pan one kiss. By Zeus,
How beautiful this soft and waving hair
(Not like my bristling curls) !—how it creeps round
Your shining shoulders, by the zephyr stirred,
As if it loved them ! I can scarcely keep
My fingers from those shoulders' sweeps and curves.
My arms desire to clasp that lithe slight waist.
One kiss—one kiss—I will—nay, throw not back
That chin and throat, and, with that rosy mouth
Laugh as you push me off. I must—I will.
You make me mad. My very fingers itch.
Come, or I'll butt my head against this tree,
And poor old Pan's pipes will be heard no more.

Don't laugh at me, and kick me in the breast
With those white feet; I'll bite them if you do!
You wilful minx, have pity on old Pan—
Have pity, or I'll seize you round the waist,
And, whether you will or not, I'll have my kiss.

MARCUS AURELIUS

TO

LUCIUS VERUS.

[*Dedicated to the Lady William Russell.*]

I HAVE received your letter, read it through
With careful thought, and, to confess the truth,
I deem it timid to a point beyond
What suits an Emperor,—timid in a way
Unsuited to the temper of the time.
You say Avidius hates us; does not stint
His jests and sneers at what we are and do;
Has no respect for the imperial robes;
Says you are an old woman, whose bald talk
You deem profound philosophy, while I

Am merely a debauched and studious fool.
You bear him no ill-will for this, you say,
(My noble Lucius, this is worthy you!)
But then you add you fear he has designs
To do us wrong, and beg me to keep watch,
Lest he, by all his wealth and power, at last
Compass our ruin. But consider this—
If to Avidius Destiny decree
The Empire's purple, all our art is vain!
You know the saying of your ancestor,
Our austere Trajan, "Never was there prince
Who killed his own heir;" no man e'er prevailed
Him to o'erthrow whom the immortal gods
Had marked as his successor: so, as well,
He whom the gods oppose must surely fall,
Not through our act, but by his destiny,
Caught in the inevitable snare of fate.

Again, the traitor or the criminal,
Though by the clearest proof convicted, stands
As 'twere at bay; one weak and friendless man
Against the State's compacted law and might,

And thus moves pity—seeming, as it were,
From that unequal match to suffer wrong.
"Wretched, indeed" (as your grandfather said),
"The fate of princes who make good their charge
Of purposed murder by their martyrdom,
Proving the plot against their life, by death."
Domitian 'twas, in truth, who spake these words,
Yet rather would I call them Hadrian's,
Since tyrants' sayings, true howe'er they be,
Have not the weight of good and noble men's.

As for Avidius, then, let him work out
His secret course, being, as you say he is,
Austere in discipline, a leader brave,
And one the State cannot afford to lose;
Let him continue there upon the edge
Of Daphnic luxury, near by Antioch,
To rein the army in and hold it firm,
Secure that Nemesis awaits on him,
As on us all, whate'er we are or do:
And for my children's interests, and mine,
If they can only be subserved by wrong,

Perish my children, rather than through wrong
They triumph! If Avidius deserve
Better than they, and if through him the State
Glory and strength superior may gain,
Better he live and win the prize he seeks!
Better they die and yield to him the State!

Please God, that while the imperial robes I wear
No blood be shed for me,—for I would fain
Be called "The Bloodless," like our Antonine!
And if this man have injured me, and shown
Ingratitude, that meanest of all sins,
At least he cannot rob me of one boon
I hold the greatest given by victory,
That of forgiveness. Ever since the Fates
Placed me upon the throne, two aims have I
Kept fixed before my eyes; and they are these:—
Not to revenge me on my enemies,
And not to be ungrateful to my friends.

A SONG OF ISRAEL.

OUR Christ shall come in glory and in power,
    Born to command.
He shall not weep or pray, or cringe or cower,
But with God's lightnings in His hand
    Tremendous there shall stand.

All eyes shall drop before His awful face
    In doubt and dread;
When He shall come, the Saviour of our race,
The crown of triumph on His head,
    Even as the Prophets said.

The sharp sword of His vengeance He shall wield
    To smite and slay.
Justice shall be His weapon and our shield;
And all who dare to disobey
    His breath shall sweep away.

His hand shall wipe away their griefs and woes,
    Who cling to Him.
His wrath like chaff shall scatter all their foes;
His power shall build Jerusalem
    With sounding song and hymn.

The hand and thought of man shall quail before
    That shape august;
And prostrate every face to earth adore
Him in whose balance we are dust,
    The mighty King—the Just.

Then shall the song of triumph once again
    For us be heard,
And Israel's children sound the joyous strain,
The Christ has come—the King and Lord—
    The Wonderful—the Word.

A PRIMITIVE CHRISTIAN IN ROME.

[*Dedicated to T. G. A.*]

It seems so strange to us of the new faith,
Who feel its beauty, joy, and holiness,
Rising above this lower Pagan creed,
Like morning o'er the dark and dreaming earth;
To us who have beheld, known, talked with those
Who walked beside our Lord, and heard his voice,
And with their own eyes saw his miracles,—
To hear these Romans, Marcus, Caius—nay,
Even Lucius, who is learned, liberal, trained
In every school of thought, deny them all:
Calling them mere impostures, or at best,
Distortions of the facts, half true, half false,
With nothing but the false miraculous!

It makes us grieve, as showing how they lack
That sense by which alone the natural man,
As Paul says, can receive the things of God.
But when had any Roman in all time
A spiritual sense? 'Tis to the East
The power of prophecy is given: alone
It shapes religions, has the inner sight
That through the matter sees the soul beyond,
Is through its faith receptive, not its mind,
And nearer unto God, as is the child.
The West, immersed in things, is as the man,
And joys to fashion governments and laws;
It orders facts, it thinks, invents, and works,
But blind and deaf to spiritual truth
Lives in the Present, builds no infinite bridge
Into the Future, hopes not, nor divines.
At highest, 'tis the world's great intellect,
Its understanding, brain, and not its soul.
Lucius is of the West; he cannot feel
Those finer impulses beyond the sense,
Those inward yearnings stretching out of sight,
Where reason cannot follow, after truth.

As far as intellect can lead him on
Up the clear path of logic, he will go;
The rest is nonsense, and, of course, he likes
The well-trod path as being the most safe.
And thus he reasons on the miracles :—

"Of facts like these, conforming to no law,
There are a thousand chances of mistake
To one in favour of the apparent facts,—
First, self-deception; strong desire to see
Begets the power of seeing; from itself
The nervously expectant sense projects
Its image, its mirage, or hears returned
The outward echo of the inward voice;
And while the reason and the judgment drowse,
The fancy all alive, sees, hears, accepts.
Then come illusions of the senses;—Facts
Half seen are wholly false,—scarce facts at all.
Let but the fact be strange and new, surprise
Destroys the power of scrutiny.—Again,
Wonder, the habitual state of many minds,
(Those, most of all, religiously inclined),

Love of the marvellous, a dread to peer
Too keenly into that which wears a garb
Of holiness, a proneness to revere
What others reverence—all lead astray.
Belief is passive: it receives, accepts;
But doubt is active: it disputes, rejects.
You think these wonders, facts. You say that Christ
Was holy in his aspect, pure in life,
And in his perfectness above mankind.
I will not question this: I only say
He was a man, at best, and not a god.
The Jews could not have crucified a god.
No, nor a demigod, like Hercules.

"Observe, I do not say as others do,
That he was wicked in intent, and sought
A kingly crown above his wretched tribe.
And if he did, I care not. What he said
Was well enough, only it was not new.
All that is good is found in Socrates,
Or Plato, or the old Philosophies.
Had he been born in Greece, he might, perhaps,

Have graced the train of one of these great men.
But in that dismal Syria, 'mid a herd
Of ignorant Jews, most of them fishermen,
Who worshipped him, he lost all common sense.
From what I hear, he grew half-cracked at last,
And thought himself a god, and claimed the power
Of miracles, like other madmen here.
Well, well; he suffered for all that by death,
And, I daresay, was better than the most
Among that loathsome people. For all that,
Touched in his brain he was, you must admit.
For what man in his senses ever dreamed
He from the dead should rise with pomp and power
A kingdom to establish on the earth?

"As for his miracles, I do not doubt
That some among that herd of credulous fools,
On whom he practised, thought they saw these things.
But who was there with eyes and mind well trained
To sift the facts, to judge the evidence,
To question, to examine, to record?
Not one; the stupid crowd cried 'miracle'

(For everything is miracle to them);
The Scribes and Pharisees, the learned men,
All stood aloof and scorned him and his works.

"And were they true, what prove they?—Why, in Rome
These wonder-working magians come by scores,
Each with his new inspired theogony,
Each with his miracle to prove him God!
For instance, there is Judas, whom they call
The Gaulonite; and his three sons as well;
There is Menander, and Cerinthus too,
Theudas, and the greatest two of all,
Simon of Gitton, named the Magian,
And Apollonius of Tyana.
Thousands assert for them, as you for Christ,
A supernatural power, a gift divine.
What shall I say? All surely are not gods!
No! nor a single one. Some, as I hear,
Are scholars versed in Egypt's mystic lore,
And by the subtle thought of Greece imbued,
With minds enriched by travel and strange tongues,
And skilled in writing, teaching, prophecy;

'Tis even said their prophecies prove true ;
If so, by chance, by happy guess, no more.
Yet if I hold these miracles of theirs
As mere delusions (and you say they are),
How can you ask me to accept on faith
Those Christ (a good man, if you will, but yet
An untaught Jew of Galilee) performed,
Far out of sight, with none to vouch for them
Except a ruck of wretched ignorant Jews?
As for their doctrines, systems, forms of faith,
There is an Eastern likeness in them all,
Simon or Christ—'tis nearly the same thing.

" And so this magian had the power, you think,
To drive out shrieking devils from the breasts
Of madmen, and compel them by his will
To rush into a herd of guiltless swine ;
Nay, that he cured the sick, and raised the dead,
One Lazarus, four days buried, till he stank ;
Even more, that he could raise himself to life
When crucified and dead, and in his tomb ;
And all because these awe-struck vulgar Jews

Saw some one like him, and affirmed 'twas he.
A woman first, a Mary Magdalene,
Set all these stories going. Who was she?
A half-mad courtesan, one who had owned
Her seven devils—but of her the less
You say the better. You'll at least admit
The kingdom that he promised on the earth,
The pomp, the power, the glory, were all trash.
He vanished very swiftly out of sight
For all his promises, and left the fools
Who trusted him to gape and stare to see
Some day the heavens open, as he said,
And him with angels coming. When he comes
Pray give me notice;—I, too, will believe;
Till then, excuse me; on such evidence
Of such grave portents, I to change my faith!
I would not hang a sparrow on it all."

So Lucius thinks, and talks, and never sees
How strange a contradiction in him lies;
For he believes in all the wildest myths,
And miracles, and wonders of his gods,

Ay, and his demigods as well, and pays
To them his reverential sacrifice.
Like a good pagan, he believes them all,
Though he admits, of course, he never saw,
Nor any eyes of any living man;
Though all the evidence is far away,
Dimmed and obscured by misty centuries;
And though these myths are vouched by writings vague
Or by tradition only, differing, too,
In each tradition. Yet this faith being fixed,
Established by long ages of belief,
It must be true; and our good Lucius sees
In all these variations proofs of truth.
The facts remain, he says, despite them all,
Coloured by this report or that report,
For this is human merely—only shows
How various minds are variously impressed;
One sees the fact as red, one green, one blue,
But all this difference proves the existing fact.

But when Christ comes within our very reach,
And living crowds behold his miracles,

Attesting them by strenuous belief,
And sudden cries, and life-long change of faith,
All were deceived; such strange things cannot be!
Yet either they were true or false. If false,
How were these crowds impressed to think they saw
What never happened? Is not this as strange,
As wondrous as the miracles themselves?
"Tricks, tricks," he says, "they only thought they saw;
Do not a juggler's tricks deceive us all?
I have no faith in Apollonius
For all the evidence—it must be trick.
In ancient times the gods came down to man,
Assuming human powers—but that is past;
But when a human creature of to-day
Assumes their functions, and works miracles
Against the laws of nature, and calls up
The dead, the best thing is to hold him mad."

No! Lucius will not try the old and new
By the same test; a kind of mystery shrouds
The ancient fact; the current of belief
For generations carries him along.

The early faith, stamped on his childish mind,
Can never be erased—'tis deep as life.
The priest, the sacrifice, the daily rites,
The formula, the fashion, the old use
Possess him, colouring all his life and thought;
And we, who in the new, pure faith rejoice,
Seem to his eyes, at least, but fools misled,
Who only seek his gods to overthrow,
And to whom ruin in the end must come.
We smile in pity—let us, too, be just.
'Tis hard to root up all one's faith at once;
All the old feelings, all the happy dreams,
All the sweet customs, the long growth of years.
The very superstitions of our youth
Have fragrance in them. Underneath the words,
We faltered clinging to a mother's hand,
A dim, sweet music flows. To that old song
No new-writ verse will ever run so smooth.

We strike his faith, and whoso strikes our faith
We hold as foe—and oft lose sight of Truth
Defending dogmas, doctrines, formulas,

Shells though they be, from which the life has fled.
While yet the mind is plastic to a touch,
The die of doctrine strikes, deep in, our faith,
And age but hardens the impression there.
Half our fixed notions are but ancient ruts
Of empty words and formulas of thought,
Worn in by repetition and long use—
And easy run the wheels within these ruts.
He who assails and goads the mind to think,
Or starts it from the grooves of prejudice,
We call foul names, we hate, we scorn, we fear;
He seems at once a foe to man and God.
What will he do? Old superstitious props
Hold up our lives; if they be stricken down,
What shall befall us? Oh! that way lies death!
Old miracles, myths, dogmas, all things old,
Are reverent for their age. It is the new
We have to fear: as if God did not work
With fresh abounding power in our own day,
In our own souls; as if dead creeds could hold
The living spirit, and these pagan husks
For ever feed the soul that starves for Truth.

I will not say but in old myths resides
Something of good—some tender living germ
Of beauty and delight. Though I renounce
Their errors for this higher, holier life
That Christ has given; still 'tis sweet to think
Of Aphrodite rising from the sea,
The incarnate dream of beauty; of the staid,
Calm dignity of wisdom bodied forth
In grand Minerva; of the gracious joy,
The charm of nature, Bacchus represents;
Of Flora scattering flowers and breathing spring;
Of all those lovely shapes that lurking gleam
Through nature's sunny openings. Ah! I know
Reason rejects them for a higher thought,
And yet, at times, that old sweet faith returns
To tempt me back in its poetic train.
At times, the one Eternal Father seems
So far away, and this fair world that teemed
With airy shapes, so void and cold and bare.

But this is folly. Yet if in my heart
Old superstitions still possess a charm,

How harshly blame our Lucius, who remains
Fixed in the old—to whom we only seem
Rash innovators, bringing in new gods?

Of other stuff is our friend Caius made.
The folly of this faith he will admit;
"And yet," he says, "the system stands our stead
Despite its follies—why then cast it down?
Truth is impossible; we cannot know;
The impenetrable veil of destiny
Behind our life, before our life is dropped.
All is an idle guess, and this mixed creed
Of superstitions has its gleams of truth.
It served our fathers; if we cast it down
Then chaos comes. Thinking results at last
In wretchedness. We cannot hope to know.
Only the gods know. Man's mind must be fed
With superstitions mixed with truth; pure truth
Would merely madden; for as we are made
Half mind, half matter, so our thoughts must be.
Then let our faith stand where it is; the beams
Are rotten here and there, but he who mends

May topple down the temple on our heads,
And leave us godless. Nay, the parasite
Of superstition, like the ivy, knits
The old wall's crumbling stones. For higher minds
A higher truth, a purer faith—but *that*
Through all these forms, we, who have eyes, can see,
The forms themselves the common herd demand.
Since all at last is theory, the best
Is to be happy, calm, and confident.
What is, is—and we cannot alter it.
Then plague me not with revelations new.
All things are revelations; every creed
Comes from above, from God, from all the gods.
Pure sunlight blinds the eye, so comes it veiled
With soft suffusion in the ambient air;
The sun, itself one speck—the positive
Set in an infinite negative of sky,
And beauty, offspring of the eternal light,
Dimmed to soft hues to suit our mortal sense.

"As for your miracles, I heed them not;
For all things, in one sense, are miracles.

Who can explain the simplest fact of life,
As how we see, or move our hand, or speak,
Or how we think, or what is life or death.
By dint of daily doing use wears out
All strangeness; and with words which but restate
And group the facts, we fancy we explain.
Our so-called laws of nature are but rules
Drawn by experience from recurrent facts,
Which every new phenomenon corrects.
Cause and effect are only cheating words;
We know no causes, we but see effects.
Yet, as in one sense all is miracle,
So, in another, no such thing exists.
The new, the strange, outside the common rule
Of man's experience, seems miraculous,
For mortal eyes are dim, and short of sight.
But could we through this world's phenomena
Pierce to the essence and the life of things,
All would arrange itself to perfect law—
No breaches, no exceptions, all pure law."

Our Decimus, who hopes to win the rank

Of tribune, takes a somewhat different view.
"Don't talk to me," he says, "of right or wrong,
Of true or false, we all must take the world
For what it is. Against established things
Why run your head, and spoil your chance in life?
Christ may have been a god, or he may not,
But here in Rome we worship other gods;
Better or worse is not the question here.
If you would win success, go with the crowd,
Nor like a fool against the current strive;
What will you gain by warring with the time,
And preaching doctrines that the general mind
Considers impious? Even were they true,
They only raise up foes to tread you down.
As for myself, I'm not the babbling fool
To utter all I think. I sacrifice
With all the rest, perform the common rites,
And do the thing that's deemed respectable;
And so I win the favour of all men.
What care I if the crowd be right or wrong?
I use them just to serve my purposes,
As steps whereby to rise to place and power.

One should not be the last to leave the old,
Nor yet the first to welcome in the new.
The popular belief—that is my faith;
My gods are always on the side that wins."

Marcus, the augur, whose whole life is spent
In omens, auguries, and sacrifice,
And service at the temple in white robes,
So deep is sunken in the pagan rut
He cannot start his mind even to think.
Our creed to him is rank impiety,
Worthy of death. He to the beasts would throw
Whoever dares our doctrines to embrace.
His faith is absolute; no shade of doubt
Has ever crossed him; he is planted there
Firm as a tree, or rather, like a wall;
A tree lives, grows, but he is simply dead,
Stone upon stone, dull, dead, fixed, like a wall.
Thus, buttressed up by custom's honoured props,
Established in the faith of centuries,
Engraved with mystic lines and Orphean hymns,
Old saws and sacred lore of ancient priests,

An honest, absolute, stolid wall he stands,
Firm to uphold the statues of the gods,
And shield them from the assaults of impious men.
If I beseech him to consider well
And reason on his faith, he cries, amazed,
" Reason ! what more fallacious guide than that?
Reason ! with human reason do you dare
To explain the gods, and to assail our faith?
They in the days of old revealed themselves,
Assumed our shapes, ordained the sacrifice
Of blood and wine upon our altars poured,
Their power attested by miraculous deeds,
And still by omens, portents, auguries,
Inform and aid us on our human path.
You do not understand them? oh, indeed!
And so you summon them before your bar,
Bid them explain their doings and their laws,
And if they fail to meet your views, why, then
You judge them and reject them. Oh, I see!
The gods must ask leave to be gods from us,
And beg our pardon if by ways obscure,
Instead of common human ways, they work,

Or else we will arise and get new gods.
Oh, Jupiter! who are these impious men?
Whence do they come, what do they mean, who thus
Set up at Rome their superstitions vile,
And with their feeble reason dare oppose
The will of heaven? Go, atheist, infidel,
Go, and ask pardon of the gods, and learn
Obedience, and humility, and fear,
Or Jove himself will from his right hand launch
His thunderbolt, and sweep you to your fate."

At times, this solid, settled faith of his
Shakes me with doubt. For what if he be right,
And this new faith that so commends itself
To all I am and hope, be, at the worst,
Temptation and delusion, shall I set
My face against the verdict of the world?
Shall not the faith that soothed the dying bed
Of Socrates—the faith that Plato taught
And Cicero avowed, suffice for me?
Shall I dare question what such minds affirm?
"Obey! Obey!" a voice within me cries

('Tis the old echo of my early faith),
And then, "Arouse!" cries out a stronger voice,
"Arouse! shake off this torpor! Sink not down
In the old creed—easy because 'tis old;
In the dead faith—so fixed, because 'tis dead."

Let us go in and speak with Paul again.
He is so strong, he braces up our faith,
And stiffens all the sinews of the mind.

ORESTES.

How tranquil is the night! how calm and deep
This sacred silence! Not an olive-leaf
Is stirring on the slopes; all is asleep—
All silent, save the distant drowsy streams
That down the hillsides murmur in their dreams.
The vast sad sky all breathless broods above,
And peace and rest this solemn temple steep.
Here let us rest—it is the hour of love—
Forgetting human pain and human grief.

But see! half-hidden in the columned shade,
Who panting stands, with hollow eyes dismayed,

That glance around as if they feared to see
Some dreaded shape pursuing? Can it be
Orestes, with those cheeks so trenched and worn—
That brow with sorrow seamed, that face forlorn?
Ay, 'tis Orestes! we are not alone.
What human place is free from human groan?
Ay, 'tis Orestes! In the temple there,
Refuge he seeks from horror, from despair.
Look! where he listens, dreading still to hear
The avenging voices sounding in his ear—
The awful voices that, by day and night,
Pursue relentless his despairing flight.
Ah! vain the hope to flee from Nemesis!
He starts—again he hears the horrent hiss
Of the fierce Furies through the darkness creep.
And list! along the aisles the angry sweep,
The hurrying rush of trailing robes—as when,
Through shivering pines asleep in some dim glen,
Fierce Auster whispers. Yes, even here they chase
Their haunted victim—even this sacred place
Stays not their fatal footsteps. As they come,
Behold him with that stricken face of doom

Fly to the altar, and there falling prone,
Strike with his brow Apollo's feet of stone.
"Save me!" he cries; "Apollo! hear and save;
Not even the dead will sleep in their dark grave.
They come—the Furies! To this tortured breast
Not even night, the calm, the peaceful, can give rest.
Stretch forth thy hand, great God! and bid them
cease.
Peace, oh Apollo! give the victim peace!"

See! the white arm above him seems to wave,
And all at once is silent as the grave,
And sleep stoops down with noiseless wings outspread,
And brooding hovers o'er Orestes' head;
And like a gust that roars along the plain
Seaward, and dies far off, so dies the pain,
The deep remorse, that long his life hath stung,
And he again is guiltless, joyous, young.
Again he plays, as in the olden time,
Through the cool marble halls, unstained by crime.
Hope holds his hands, joy strikes the sounding strings,
Love o'er him fluttering shakes his purple wings,

And sorrow hides her face, and dark death creeps
Into the shade, and every Fury sleeps.

Sleep! sleep, Orestes! let thy torments cease!
Sleep! great Apollo grants thy prayer for peace.
Sleep! while the dreams of youth around thee play,
And the fierce Furies rest.—Let *us* away.

TO FORTUNE.

OH Goddess! fixed and fair and calm,
That bearest in thy grasp the palm—
That bearest in thy grasp the rod—
Oh voice of Fate! oh smile of God!—

Be gracious—lend to us thy ear—
Be not too awful, too austere.
Against thy will no power avails;
Without thy aid all struggle fails.

Stayed by thy hand, no reed so spare
But, column-like, life's weight will bear;
Reft of thy hand our steps to lead,
The brazen shaft is like a reed.

Blow but thy breath across the sea,
Our galleys go triumphantly;
Avert thy face, though skies are fair
We sink and founder in despair.

Dear Goddess, turn to us thy face!
Not justice we implore, but grace;
Give us what none can win or buy—
Thy godlike gift, prosperity.

PRAXITELES AND PHRYNE.

[Dedicated to R. B.]

A THOUSAND silent years ago,
The twilight faint and pale
Was drawing o'er the sunset glow
Its soft and shadowy veil;

When from his work the Sculptor stayed
His hand, and turned to one
Who stood beside him, half in shade,
Said, with a sigh, "'Tis done.

"Thus much is saved from chance and change,
That waits for me and thee;

Thus much—how little!—from the range
  Of Death and Destiny.

"Phryne, thy human lips shall pale,
  Thy rounded limbs decay,—
Nor love nor prayers can aught avail
  To bid thy beauty stay;

"But there thy smile for centuries
  On marble lips shall live,—
For Art can grant what love denies,
  And fix the fugitive.

"Sad thought! nor age nor death shall fade
  The youth of this cold bust;
When this quick brain and hand that made,
  And thou and I art dust!

"When all our hopes and fears are dead,
  And both our hearts are cold,
And love is like a tune that's played,
  And Life a tale that's told,

" This senseless stone, so coldly fair,
That love nor life can warm,
The same enchanting look shall wear,
The same enchanting form.

" Its peace no sorrow shall destroy;
Its beauty age shall spare
The bitterness of vanished joy,
The wearing waste of care.

" And there upon that silent face
Shall unborn ages see
Perennial youth, perennial grace,
And sealed serenity.

" And strangers, when we sleep in peace,
Shall say, not quite unmoved,
So smiled upon Praxiteles
The Phryne whom he loved."

MARCUS ANTONIUS.

[*Dedicated to L. C.*]

'TIS vain, Fonteus!—As the half-tamed steed,
Scenting the desert, lashes madly out,
And strains and storms and struggles to be freed,
Shaking his rattling harness all about—
So, fiercer for restraint, here in my breast
Hot passion rages, firing every thought;
For what is honour, prudence, interest
To the wild strength of love? Oh best of life,
My joy, hope, triumph, glory, my soul's wife,
My Cleopatra! I desire thee so
That all restraint to the wild winds I throw.

Come what come will, come life, come death, to me
'Tis equal, if again I look on thee.
Away, Fonteus! tell her that I rage
With madness for her. Nothing can assuage
The strong desire, the torment, the fierce stress
That whirls my thoughts round, and inflames my brain,
But her great ardent eyes—dark eyes, that draw
My being to them with a subtle law
And an almost divine imperiousness.
Tell her I do not live until I feel
The thrill of her wild touch, that through each vein
Electric shoots its lightning; and again
Hear those low tones of hers, although they steal
As by some serpent-charm my will away,
And wreck my manhood.

Oh! Octavia,

This lying galls me—this poor mean pretence
Of love—this putting every word to school—
When all at best is blank indifference.
Even hate for you is only cold and dull—
I hate you that I cannot hate you more.
Were you but savage, wicked to the core,

Less pious, prudish, prudent, made to rule,
I might have loved or hated more; but now
Nothing on earth seems half so deadly chill
As your insipid smile and placid brow,
Your glacial goodness and proprieties.

Tell my dear serpent I must see her—fill
My eyes with the glad light of her great eyes,
Though death, dishonour, anything you will,
Stand in the way! Ay, by my soul! disgrace
Is better in the sun of Egypt's face
Than pomp or power in this detested place.
Oh for the wine my queen alone can pour
From her rich nature! Let me starve no more
On this weak tepid drink that never warms
My life-blood: but away with shams and forms!
Away with Rome! One hour in Egypt's eyes
Is worth a score of Roman centuries.
Away, Fonteus! Tell her, till I see
Those eyes I do not live—that Rome to me
Is hateful,—tell her—oh! I know not what—
That every thought and feeling, space and spot

Is like an ugly dream, where she is not;
All persons plagues; all doing wearisome;
All talking empty; all these feasts and friends—
These slaves and courtiers, princes, palaces—
This Cæsar, with his selfish aims and ends,
His oily ways and sleek hypocrisies—
This Lepidus; and, worse than all by far,
This mawkish, pious, prude Octavia—
Are bonds and fetters, tedious as disease,
Not worth the parings of her finger-nails.

Oh for the breath of Egypt!—the soft nights
Of the voluptuous East—the dear delights
We tasted there—the lotus-perfumed gales
That dream along the low shores of the Nile,
And softly flutter in the languid sails!
Oh for the queen of all!—for the rich smile
That glows like autumn over her dark face—
For her large nature—her enchanting grace—
Her arms, that are away so many a mile!
Away, Fonteus!—lose no hour—make sail—
Weigh anchor on the instant—woo a gale

To blow you to her. Tell her I shall be
Close on your very heels across the sea,
Praying that Neptune send me storms as strong
As Passion is, to sweep me swift along,
Till the white spray sing whistling round my prow,
And the waves gurgle 'neath the keel's sharp plough.
Fly, fly, Fonteus! When I think of her
My soul within my body is astir!
My wild blood pulses, and my hot cheeks glow!
Love with its madness overwhelms me so
That I—oh! go, I say! Fonteus, go!——

MODERN

o

GIANNONE.

[*Dedicated to E. S.*]

TAKE a cigar—draw up your chair,
There's at least a good half-hour to spare
Before the Capuchin clock strikes one,
And the bell, with a sharp spasmodic tinkle,
Rouses the Fràti to shuffle to prayer,
And the altar candles begin to twinkle
In the cheerless chapel, bleak and bare—
By Jove! we are better off here than there.
And now, as that *friend* of yours has gone,
There's a word I must whisper to you, alone.

Friends grow dearer, and hearts draw nearer,
Calmed in the silent centre of night;

And words we may say, that the full mid-day,
If it should hear us, would jeer outright.
Day, with its din, for distrust and doubt!
Night for confidence, friendship, love!
The day's work done, and the world shut out,
The streets all silent, the stars above,
Pleasant it is to gather about
The fire of wood, and muse and dream,
And talk of the hopes and joys of youth,
And open our hearts and confess the truth,
Ceasing to make-believe and seem.

Fling another log on the fire,
Another log from the Sabine hill,
And a heap of those rusty crackling canes
That out on the sunny Campagna plains
Held on their trellis the grape-hung vine,
Whose blood was drained for this purple wine,
Our straw-enwoven fiasco to fill.
Look! the old tendrils, stiff as wire,
Cling to them still with their strong desire,
Outlasting death—as our friendship will.

How the flame bickers, and quivers, and flickers,
Darting its eager tongues about!
Then blazes abroad with genial flashes,
Till the sap comes singing and bubbling out.
Wild as a Mœnad with myriad fancies,
Hither and thither it leaps and dances,
Fitful, whimsical, glad, and free,
Like a living thing with a heart and soul.
Oh, the wood-fire is the fire for me!
Away with your heartless mechanical coal,
Your vulgar drudge, so sullen and slow,
That ne'er with a flame of fancy flashes,
But burns with a grim and business glow,
And crumbles away to dirty ashes,
And smells of the furnace and factory.
Talk of the home and hearth! of late
Nothing we've had but house and grate—
Nothing in England to warm to the core,
Like the vast old chimneys and fires of yore,
When the great logs blazed with a genial roar.

Hark to that mossy log, whose heart

The contadino has cloven apart,
Singing its death-song! How it tells
What the cicadæ chirped in the dells,
When it was young, and its leafy pride
Shadowed Pan with its branches wide;
And what old Auster, bluff and bold,
Screamed in its ear while it shivered with cold.
Thousands of idyls it has to sing,
Of love and summer, of youth and spring;
Of the Dryad that slipt with her rustling dress
Into its murmurous leafiness;
Of the rout of Bacchanals, ivy-crowned,
Shaking the air with the cymbal's sound,
While the yawning panther's velvet foot
Pressed the rank grasses over its root;—
Of the timorous Naiad, pearled with dew,
That fled to the bubbling torrent near,
And, hid by the bushes, looked trembling through
At the smooth-limbed Bacchus, in love and fear;
Of the chance and change of the season's spell,
Of musical birds and odorous flowers,
Of the storm that swept like a chorded shell

The groaning forest—of whispering showers,
Of all that, rooted there, it beheld,
Since first in its veins the young sap swelled.
But what like this has your coal to tell?
Black old mummy; what has it known,
Since the earth was a bubbling lava-vat,
Sunk in its dreary silent tomb,
But the earthquake's rumbling sound of doom,
Till it leapt to light with a split and groan,
With a toad, perhaps, encased in its stone—
How can you warm your heart at that?

How the wood blazes! Fill my glass!
This Lacryma Christi goes to the heart,
And makes the olden memories start,
Like an April rain on last year's grass.
How the days go! how the hours pass!
Sometimes like a thousand years it seems,
And then like a little month of dreams,
Since the Odes of Horace you taught me to scan,
And helped me over Homeric crevasses,
I, stumbling along where you lightly ran,

By the shores of the Poluphloisboio Thalasses—
Then how I longed to be a man,
Though thrilling with all a boy's joy of the lasses,
With my crown just even with your shoulder,
Looking with reverence up to you—
Longing to know the things you knew,
You six feet high and six years older,
And leaping over with quiet ease
What brought me staggering on to my knees.
Then I remember you went to Rome,
And on the hem of your garment brought
Odours back to our quiet home,
That ravished with sweetness my boyish thought.
How your talk, like an o'erbrimmed cup,
Ran over with beauty, my heart drank up;—
Oranges, olives—tinkling guitars,
Skies all throbbing with palpitant stars,
Moonlighted terraces, gardens, and groves,
Bubbling of nightingales, cooing of doves—
Portia's, Laura's, and Juliet's loves,—
Everything lovely I seemed to see
When you were talking of Italy;

There you almost seemed to have met
Titian, Raffaelle, Tintoret,
And felt the grasp of Angelo's hand,
And known Da Vinci, so calm and grand,
And walked in that glorious company,
Whose starry names are above us seen
Like constellations in the sky;
And you in that marble world had been,
Where the Grecian and Roman gods still reign,
And lord it in Art's serene domain;
And behind the veil of talk you wove,
Their figures, half-hidden, seemed to move,
And, beckoning, smile—to pass away
At a single touch of my everyday.

Ah! the old dreams—old times—old joys—
Buried beyond the Present's noise,
How still they sleep beneath time's river!
All of their sorrows and pains forgot,
All of their beauty, without a blot,
Living to perfume the memory for ever.

Well! once you filled my heart with wine,
That made me drunk with a life divine;
And I pour into yours, as a recompense,
Small beer of advice and common sense.
You were a poet to me at home,
I'll be a preacher to you in Rome.

So, to come out of this dreamy land,
To the business matter of fact in hand;
You know that fellow that just went out—
But pray, do you know his business here?—
How he is living—what he's about,
Here in Rome this many a year?
Somebody introduced him? He seems
A sort of a pious good-natured fool,—
A convert, they told you, with dreams and schemes
For the Church's universal rule ?
All very well; but what are his means?
Faith is lovely, but is not food;—
The heart has its pulse, but the stomach needs beans,
And texts don't do when the appetite's rude.
Man's but a poor weak creature at best,

Till the fiend in the belly is lulled to rest.
Throw *him* his dose, and the road is free
For meditation and sanctity.
Now look me, my old friend, straight in the eye—
Unless appearances grossly lie
(I'm as sorry to say it as you to hear,
But after midnight one must be sincere),
That fellow 's only a Government Spy!
Of course you're surprised.—There's nothing on earth
So base in your eyes as a Government Spy;
He's half an Englishman, too, by birth,
So the thing is an impossibility.
Be calm, my friend, that's the way it looks
To us poor sinners; but we mistake:
The law is different in his looks;—
He acts for the Holy Church's sake;
And there's nothing so dirty you may not do,
With absolution and blessing too—
Not to speak of the money part—
If the Church's good you have at heart.
Holy fictions are never lies;
'Tis the pious purpose purifies.

And pray distinguish, if you please,
Those who, like martyrs, sacrifice
Instincts of commonest decencies,
Seeking to win an immortal prize
From merely common vulgar spies.
Spirito Santo's not the same
As Aqua Vitæ, even in name.
Spirito Santo mumbles and prays
The while his friend to death he betrays;
Aqua Vitæ is bought and sold,
And frankly admits that he works for gold.
For, "Bah!" he says, "a man must live,
And holes there are in every one's sieve.
Nobody's pure as he pretends,
And we all eat dirt for our selfish ends.
Pride is the ruin of angel and man;
All of us do as well as we can;
You at my dirty business scoff,
But silver spoons are found in the trough.
Cheaper than you I am, I'll admit,
Because I am poorer, not worse a whit.
A beggar's sole chance is to sleep in a ditch;

I'd be respectable too—were I rich ;
But calling names don't break any bones,
And eggs are eggs, though you call them stones."

Talk as vulgar as this your friend
Is ready as you to reprehend :
For, "Ah !" he says, "we cannot refuse
Our crosses and burdens, though hard to bear :
The world's always ready to sneer and abuse,
But we must answer their scoffs with a prayer :
Our duty is not for us to choose.
Fallible reason to man is given ;
The Church alone has the keys to heaven ;
She only knows what is purest and best,
And her servants humbly must do her behest.
She doeth a mighty good with a fool,
And, using me as a worthless tool,
If I mistake, and stumble, and fall,
She shall give absolution for all."

Now I may be deceived, and I hope I am ;
But a wolf may borrow the fleece of a lamb,

And I fear your friend is that kind of sham.
But listen, I 'll spin a yarn for you,
And every thread of it's simply true ;
And then you can come to your own decision,
If I'm right or wrong in my suspicion.

'Tis years, as you know, that I've lived in Rome,
Till now it's familiar to me as home ;
And 'tis years ago I knew Giannone,
A capital fellow, with great black eyes,
And a pleasant smile of frank surprise,
And as gentle a pace as a lady's pony,
Ready to follow wherever you bid ;
His oaths were, "Per Bacco !" and "Dio mio !"
And "Guardi !" he cried to whatever you said ;
But though not overfreighted with esprit or *brio*,
His heart was better by far than his head.
His education was rather scanty ;
But what on earth could he have done
With an education, having one,
Unless he chose for the scarlet to run,
And study the Fathers and lives of the Santi ?

Nevertheless, I know he had read,
Because he quoted them, Tasso and Dante;
And so often he recommended the prosy
Promessi Sposi, I must suppose he
Had also achieved that tale of Manzoni;
And besides Monte Christo and Uncle Tom,
And the history of Italy and Rome,
(For he thoroughly knew how Liberty's foot
Had been pinched, and maimed, and lamed in her
boot),
He had studied with zeal the book of the Mass,
And Libretti of all the operas.

This little learning sufficed for Giannone,
And, sooth to say, as little money;
Most of the latter he spent upon dress,
And his life was neither more nor less
Than the difficult problem, day by day,
To drive the cursèd time away.
So having nothing himself to do,
He would dawdle away your morning for you.
When you were silent to drive him away,

You missed your man—he would stay and stay,
With the same old phrases, the livelong day.
And smiling at nothing, and so content
He lounged at his ease on your sofa there,
Or peeped in your boxes without your consent,
Or paced through the room, or, pausing, stood
At the glass, and examined himself with care,
And arranged his cravat, or mustache, or hair.
And so pleased if you threw him a word or two,
That you had no heart to be downright rude,
And say, "My dear fellow, you really intrude;"
Or if at last you were ready to swear,
And cried, "I am busy; I've something to do!"
Dull as a stone to what you meant, he
Would quietly settle himself in his chair,
And smiling answer, with fatuous air,
"Faccia, senza complimenti."

His room was an armoury of swords—
Some blades scribbled with Koran words,
Some long and thin, some short and stout,
Some crooked, some straight, some curved about.

He had ancient guns and pistols too,
One-barrelled, six-barrelled, old and new,
With every species of bore and stock,
And every imaginable lock ;
Daggers, with hilts by Cellini made,
Or so at least Giannone said ;
A savage bludgeon from Southern Seas,
A Turkish scimitar's gilded blade,
An Indian tomahawk and a creese ;—
Everything murderous, terrible, wild,
Pleased this creature, so gentle and mild.
On his wall was a head of Rachel, of course,
Flanked by two dogs, a stag, and a horse
From Landseer's brush, and, poised on her neat toe,
The delicate sylph-like shape of Cerito.
On his hearth-rug lay a lion's skin,
And a couple of dogs made a terrible din,
Yelping and screaming at all that came in.
And here he lay, in his warlike den,
And made his breakfast on "café au lait,"
The very idlest of idle men,
Smoking and gaping the morning away,

And handling his pistols now and then ;
Shabby enough in his dressing-gown,
With a soiled shirt on, and his slippers down,
And a scarlet fez with a tassel blue
Perched on his head, not over-new.

But as soon as the morning he'd worried by,
The grub would change to a butterfly—
Burst from his chrysalis, and appear
Likė an English milord, with a million a-year;
And when his elaborate toilet was done,
He really fancied he looked like one.
Yet, despite his short bepocketed coat,
His mutton-chop whiskers, and well-shaved throat,
And English neck-tie, and laced-up boot,
He still was Italian from head to foot.

By slowly dressing, an hour he killed,
And then the serious duty fulfilled
Of showing himself all up and down
The Corso's length to the lazy town,

Bowing and lifting his glossy hat,
Or pausing to air his innocent chat
At the carriage of Lady this or that;
And to be English out and out,
He bought a dog-cart, and drove about,
Sitting high, with majestic pride,
A tiger behind, and a friend at his side,
And a boule-dogue staring between his knees,
As like an Englishman as two peas.
He thought so at least, if we did not;
So, up and down, at a solemn trot,
With his reins held tight, as if his steed
Were wild with spirit, blood, and breed
(Though, if the simple truth be told,
It was eighteen years since he was foaled),
He drove, white-gloved, his reverend beast,
And looked like an English Sir Smith at least.

At night he went to his opera-stall,
When there was neither a party nor ball;
And, knowing the opera all by rote,
He hummed with the tenor, soprano, or bass,

Keeping ahead by a bar or note,
And winning by half a length the race;
Or, turning around with an earnest face,
He studied the circle from ceiling to floor,
With a cheap lorgnette he had hired at the door;
Or, wandering about from box to box,
With his white cravat and his oily locks,
He played with some lady's fan and smiled,
And remarked that the weather was cold or mild;
Asked when she would receive his call—
Hoped it would be a gay Carnival;
Said Lady X. was a beautiful woman—
Heard she intended to give a ball;
Knew that young American there,
The pretty girl with a rose in her hair,
The daughter, they say, of Barnum the showman—
Would have a million dollars for *dôt;*
And half he sighed at his different lot.
And with chat like this, that offended no man,
Of people and parties and weather and wealth,
And asking of everybody's health,
He talked like any agreeable Roman.

Giannone had but an empty head—
But then the worst of him is said:
A better heart, or a readier hand,
To help in whatever was plotted and planned,
You never would see in our English land.
He sang at our parties—was ready to hop
In polka, mazurka, schottische, or galopp;
Or led the cotillon till all of the girls
Had danced in the morning, and danced out their curls,
And the tired musicians were ready to drop.
He bargained for carriages, horses, and grooms—
Hired music for balls, sent flowers to your rooms—
Arranged all the picnics, and fluttered about
At every tea-drinking party or rout—
Talked terrible French, and at times even spoke
In English, said "Yas, meese," and thought it a joke.

A "guardia nobile" was Giannone,
By which he earned sufficient money
For his gloves, shirt-buttons, boots, and hat,
Though it was scarcely enough for that.
And splendid he was on a gala-day,

With his jingling sword and scarlet coat,
And his long jack-boots and helmet gay,
When along the streets he used to trot;
And great good-luck it was to meet
Giannone when you wanted a seat
To hear the chant of the Miserere,
Or to get on the balcony high and airy,
To see the Papal procession go
Over St Peter's pavement below,
Streaming along in its gorgeous show.
And then at Carnival such bouquets—
Such beautiful bon-bons, and princely ways—
Such elegant wavings of hat and hand—
Such smiles that no one could withstand—
Such compliments, as made ours seem
Like pale skim-milk to his rich cream.
Giannone's dream was always this,
To find some beautiful English "Miss,"
With a pretty face and plenty of money,
Who should fall in love and marry Giannone.

Poor fellow! he met with a different fate,

The manner of which I will now relate,
And he caught it just through imitation
Of some of the ways of our English nation.

Travel as much as we English will,
Down to the death we are English still—
The brandy and ale that we have at home,
And the sherry and port, we must have in Rome.
These thin Italian wines, we think,
Are a wishy-washy kind of drink.
Travel we must, if only to say
We are better in England every way;
And we honestly think, when we get abroad,
That England alone was made by God,
While the rest of the earth, though nobly planned,
Was finished by some apprentice's hand.
All that's not English in our eyes
Is something to sneer at, and jeer, and despise.
As for a foreigner, it's our rule
To consider him either a knave or fool;
And our sense of a kindness by one bestowed,
Weighs on our minds like an awkward load,

Till we've asked our new acquaintance to dine,
And paid off the favour with beef and wine,
And introduced him to all our set.
So it happened that Hycombe Wycombe Brown,
Of the Sussex Wycombes, a man about town,
The nephew, you know, of Sir Hycombe Guy,
Who was slain at the storming of Alisalih,
And left his name to the Gazette,
And put our Hycombe quite at his ease
With I know not how many lacs of rupees
(And he lacked them enough till then, if you please).
Well, owing Giannone a kind of debt
For buying some horses, or some such work,
He sent him a card of defiance one day
To meet him at point of the knife—and fork,
And settle the matter without delay.
Giannone accepted of course, and then,
As Wycombe's Italian was rather weak,
He asked a few of us resident men
Who knew the language, as seconds, to speak,
And among them, slim and sleek and sly,
Was your pious friend with his balking eye.

The dinner was good, and all were merry,
And plenty there was of champagne and sherry;
And the toasts were brisk and the wine was good,
And we all took quite as much as we should.
Then we went to cards; and depend upon it,
Though our seasoned brains the drink withstood,
There was a bee in Giannone's bonnet;
But to play we went—it was only whist,
But a little mill answers for little grist,
And Giannone was soon cleaned out of all
He had saved for bouquets at Carnival,
And of course he felt a little vext,
Though "Pazienza" was still his text.

But playing's dry work, and, I'm sorry to say,
Brandy was ordered to whet the play;
And Giannone kept drinking, in imitation
Of this happy custom of our nation,
Till at last his tongue had lost its rein,
And the fire had all gone into his brain.

So he began to talk quite wild,

And spoke all his thoughts out like a child;
And secrets he ought to have kept in his breast
Plumped out of his mouth like young birds from their
nest;
And names he called, and his voice was high
As he talked of Italian liberty!
And cursed the priests as the root of all evil,
And sent the Cardinals all to the devil!
And, "Now," he cried, "they have it their way,
But every dog must have his day;
And the time will come, and that before long,
When the weak will rise and drive over the strong,
And the Tricolor over the Vatican fly,
And vivas be heard for liberty!
No more King Stork, and no more Pope Log,
Fouling Italy's boot in their bog.
Better dig with the bayonet's point our graves,
And die to be freemen, than live to be slaves!
Ah, fight we will! There is nothing good
Which must not be first baptised in blood.
Let us alone, you tricking French,
Let us alone, you Austrian sneaks,

And we will purge the Augean stench
That in Bomba's and Pius's stable reeks.
We ask no help from Gascon or Guelph,
Italia will do it alone—by herself."

When the wine is in, at times the wit
To a kindle of savage flame is lit;
And Giannone, who in his common mood
Thinks more of gloves and perfumes than blood,
Now looked and talked like a man inspired,
And his thoughts blazed up as if they were fired,
And his lamping eyes (as calm as a cow's
In his everyday) now seemed to rouse
And burn beneath his low black brows.
We looked at him in amazement then,
And said, "These Italians *au fond* are men,
Veneered with ignorance though they be,
And cowed and imbruted by slavery;
Let them be roused by war or love,
They are fiercer than any of us, by Jove!"

But all the while that Giannone let fly

These arrows of his, with a dead-cold eye
Your friend sat playing, and now and then
Gleamed up with a glance as sharp as a pen
That seemed to write down every word,
And then looked away as he had not heard;
And whenever he opened his lips, he said
Something about the game,—"You've played
A heart to my club:—we're one to six;
Yours are the honours and ours the tricks."

We were all Englishmen there, you know,
And we English to suspect are slow;
But this fellow's air and sneaking look
Were something I somehow could not brook;
So I watched him well, and at last said I
To myself, "The rascal must be a spy."

The thought like an arrow of fate struck home—
You know how these sudden conclusions come,
Beyond our reason, beyond our will,
And, lightening down with electric thrill,
Reveal in one clear and perfect flash

A world that before was doubt and gloom.
So "Zitto! Zitto! don't be so rash,
Giannone," I cried; "who knows what ear
May be listening at the door to hear?"
And then, with a laugh, and looking straight
At this *friend* of yours, with his face sedate,
I added, "Who knows but there may be
A spy even here in this company?"

If I doubted before the trade of your friend,
My doubts in a moment had their end;
For a glance came straight up into my eyes
From under his lids, half fear, half surprise,
As an adder on which you chance to tread
Starts up, and darts his tongue from his head,
And then slips swiftly into the shade.
So turning back with a look demure,
And a deprecating, pious air,
As much as to say, "We must not care,
If our purposes are but high and pure,
But quell our passions and our pride,
And bear the stigma of human shame,

Knowing the means are justified
By the noble end,"—he slowly said,
Speaking, of course, about the game,
"The trick is mine—'twas the knave I played."

Now the snakes that in Italy's bosom lie
Are the twins Suspicion and Jealousy;
And the eggs from which they creep and crawl
Are hatched in the secret confessional.
Wherever you go you may hear them hiss
'Neath the covert of studied hypocrisies.
Truth is dangerous,—eyes will spy,
And ears will hear, though nobody 's nigh;
And the safest thing is to learn to lie.
So a daily distrust is engendered and bred,
That saps one's faith in the friend most dear,
And creeps to sleep in the marriage-bed,
Till the dearest and nearest you learn to fear.

The Government never forgets the rule
That it early learns in the Church's school:
Divide and conquer—that is the way.

Threaten the weak, the frank betray;
Cajole and promise—you needn't pay.
Save your children by plying your rods,
And give up to Cæsar the things that are—God's.

And oh! my children, listen and hear—
Whatever the Church commands, revere;
And distrust men's words with a holy fear;
And wherever you go, and whatever you see,
Worship only the powers that be,
And talk no nonsense of liberty.

This is the creed that Giannone knew
Better by far than I or you;
So no sooner the dread word "Spy" I spoke,
Than his fine discourse like a pipe-stem broke;
But looking around with a startled stare,
And seeing we only were English there,
His fear dropped off like a snake's old skin,
And again with a laugh we heard him begin.

"Ah!" he cried, "there's a dirty trick
In the very word that makes me sick;

You English don't know as well as I
The slobber and slime of a Government Spy.

"Sir Birichino, permit me now
To introduce him—a *friend* of mine—
Smooth, pale, bloodless lips and brow—
A long black coat, whose rubbed seams shine—
Spots on his waistcoat of grease and wine—
A tri-cornered hat all rusty with use—
Long black coarse stockings and buckled shoes;
Ah! so polite with his bows and smiles,
And his sickening compliments and wiles,
And his little serpent venomous eyes,
And his swollen chops of beastly size.
Look at the hypocrite! There he stands,
With the unctuous palms of his dirty hands
Folded together breast-high, while he sneaks
Cringing behind them wherever he speaks;
He dares not look you straight in the eyes,
But, sidling and simpering, askance alway,
He oils you over with wheedling lies,
As the boa slimes ere he swallows his prey.

Any day you may see him, he haunts
Half the cafés and restaurants;
His eye on his paper fixed,—his ear
Gleaning the talk at the table near.
No pride in *him*,—he will lick your shoes,
Thanks you for kicking him—loves abuse—
Calls it the natural spirit of youth;
Anything's sweet to him but truth.
Drop a bad word in that fellow's way,
He picks it up as a vulture its prey;
Hating whatever is wholesome and good,
And living only on carrion food.
Let him say 'rose,' it will stink in his breath.
Many a fellow owes him his death
Just for a strong word, spoken may be
When the blood was hot and the tongue too free.
But at last he reckoned without his host,
And in throwing his dirty dice he lost;
And one morning they found him taking his rest
In the street, with a dagger stuck in his breast.
And served him right, say you and I,
It was only too easy a death for a Spy."

At this your *friend* threw down his card,
Saying, "You've won to-night, 'tis true,
But to-morrow I'll have my revenge on you."
And though these words to his friend he spoke,
He looked at Giannone so sharp and hard,
With such a sinister evil look,
That a dark suspicion in me awoke.
So the good Giannone's arm I took,
And crying, "I'm off—will you go with me?"
Took him away from the company;
And after a mile of midnight Rome,
Left him safe in his den at home.

This, you'll say, and I'll confess
Was merely suspicion—no more nor less;
Yet I could not get it out of my head
Long after I was warm in my bed,
That something might happen by-and-by
To prove this fellow was only a Spy.

Two days after I went to see
Whether Giannone would walk with me—

Two sharp bell-pulls at his door;
No answer—gone out; then one pull more,
And "Ho, Giannone, Giannone, 'tis I!"
Then slipped a slide back cautiously
From a little grated hole—"Chi è,"
From a woman's voice—"Che vuole lei?"
And a shuffle of slippers when it was known
Who "*I*" was, and that I was alone.
"And where is the Signor Padrone?" I cried.
"Ah!" with a sort of convulsive groan,
The poor old servant, sighing, replied,
"Doesn't your Signoria know—
Such times—such times—oime! oibo!
The sbirri came here yesterday,
And carried the caro padrone away;
And they've rifled his desk of letters and all,
And taken the pistols and swords from the wall,
And locked up the room with a great red seal
Put over the door; and they scared me so,
With threats if I dared in the chamber to go,
That I'm all of a tremble from head to heel;
And when the bell rang, I thought it must be

Some of the sbirri come back for me.
What it's about we none of us know,
But his mother and sisters are in such a fright,
They've been weeping and praying the livelong night.
And oh, I fear, Signore dear,
There's some dreadful political business here;
Ahime!" and she wiped away a tear.

The servant's story was all too true;
I did, of course, all there was to do,
Begged, bribed, and petitioned, but all in vain.
From that night I never saw him again.
Worse, neither I nor his family knew,
Nor will you, unless your friend explain,
And Giannone himself is as ignorant too—
What was his crime—what done—what said,
That drew this punishment down on his head.
This one fact alone we know,
That since the speech of that famous night
Giannone has vanished out of sight,
And has gone to pass a year or so,
Longer perhaps,—how can one say?—
In a building where the Government pay

His lodging and board in the kindest way.
The lodging perhaps is rather bare,
And the boarding is not the best of fare,
And the company 's queer that 's gathered there—
Made up of fellows with speech more free
Than one hears in the best society;
And some of whose notions are rather opaque
Of the laws that govern property;
So that sometimes they make a mistake
In that little distinction 'twixt *meum* and *tuum*;
But then, as the Roman laws are in Latin,
Which, even in Rome, one is not pat in,
Farther, I mean, than an Ave or Matin,
It takes a scholar to read them at all;
And supposing one *has* read thoroughly through 'em,
There's a slippery space 'twixt see 'em and do 'em,
Where Grotius himself might trip and fall.

Well,—here in this cheerful company,
Where the cushions are not of silk and satin,
And on fare one cannot honestly praise,
Our poor Giannone passes his days.
It is not precisely the place to grow fat in,

And the library 's wanting, as yet, I hear,
And I'm told that the view from the window is drear,
And the host will never allow a fire,
And, besides, has ways that are rather queer
Of locking the doors, which interfere
With the perfect freedom one might desire.
But beggars cannot be choosers, you see,
And to look a gift-horse in the mouth would be
Such a breach of manners—yet, as for me,
I cannot help wishing the end would come
Of this public hospitality,
And that poor Giannone was free to go home.
But when will *that* be? you ask me—Ah!
That is the question; Chi lo sa?
Whenever it pleases the powers that be,—
Next month—next year—next century!

Now, there are the facts for my suspicion
About your friend and his pretty profession;
They're as plain to me as two ones in addition,
And I put them all into your possession.

IL CURATO.

[*Dedicated to R. S.*]

THERE's our good curate coming down the lane,
Taking his evening walk as he is wont:
'Neath the dark ilexes he pauses now
And looks across the fields; then turning round.
As Spitz salutes me with a sharp high bark,
Advising him a stranger's neàr, he stops,
Nods, makes a friendly gesture, and then waits—
His head a little bent aside, one hand
Firm on his cane, the other on his hip—
And ere I speak he greets me cheerily.

"A lovely evening, and the well-reaped fields
Have given abundant harvest. All around

They tell me that the grain is large and full;
Peasant and landlord both of them content;
And with God's blessing we shall have, they say,
An ample vintage; scarcely anywhere
Are traces of disease among the grapes;
The olives promise well, too, as it seems.
Good grain, good wine, good oil—thanks be to God
And the Madonna, who give all things good,
And only ask from us a thankful heart!

"Yes, I have been to take my evening walk
Down to the Borgo; for, thank heaven, I still
Am stout and strong and hearty, as you see.
I still can walk my three good miles as well
As when I was but sixty, though, perhaps,
A little slower than I used; but then
I've turned my eightieth year—I have indeed!
Though you would scarce believe it. More than that,
I've never lost a tooth—all good and sound—
Look! not a single one decayed or loose—
As good to crack a nut as e'er they were.
They're the great secret of my health, I think;

Like a good mill they grind the food up well,
And keep the stomach and digestion good.

"Yes, sir! I've passed the allotted term of man,
Threescore-and-ten. I'm fourscore years, all told;
But, the Lord help us, how we old men boast!
What are our fourscore years or fivescore years
(If I should ever reach as far as that)
Compared with the eternity beyond?
Yet let us praise God for the good he gives;
All are not well and strong at fourscore years.
There's farmer Lanti with but threescore years,
See how he's racked with his rheumatic pains;
He scarce can crawl along.
Do you take snuff?

"Yes, sir! 'tis fifty years since first I came
As curate to this village—fifty years!
When I look back it scarce seems possible,
And yet 'tis fifty years last May since first
I came to live in yonder little house.
You see its red-tiled roof and loggia there

Close-barnacled upon the church, that shows
Its belfry-tower above the olive-trees.
The place is rude and rough, but there I've lived
So long, I would not change it if I could.
Old things grow dear to us by constant use;
Habit is half our nature; and this house
Fits all my uses, answers all my needs,
Just as an old shoe fits one's foot; and there
I sleep as sound with its bare floor and walls
As if its bricks were spread with carpets soft,
And all the ceilings were with frescoes gay.

"But what need I of pictures on my walls?
Out of my window every day I see
Pictures that God hath painted, better far
Than Raffaelle or Razzi—these great slopes
Covered with golden grain and waving vines
And rows of olives; and then far away
Dim purple mountains where cloud-shadows drift
Darkening across them; and beyond, the sky,
Where morning dawns and twilight lingering dies.
And then, again, above my humble roof

The vast night is as deep with all its stars
As o'er the proudest palace of the king.

"So, sir, my house is good enough for me.
I have been happy there for many years,
And there's no better riches than content;
There I've my little plot of flowers—for flowers
Are God's smile on the earth,—I could not do
Without my flowers; and there I train my vines,
Just for amusement; for the people here,
Good, honest creatures, do not let me want
For grapes and wine, howe'er the season be;
Then I've two trees of apricots, and one
Great fig-tree, that beneath my window struck
Its roots into a rock-cleft years ago,
And of itself, without my care, has grown
And thriven, till now it thrusts its leaves and figs
Into my very room. Sometimes I think
This was a gift of God to me to say,
'Behold! how out of poverty's scant soil
A life may bravely grow and bear good fruit,
And be a blessing and a help.' May I

Be like this fig-tree, by the grace of God!
I have one peach-tree, but the fruit this year
Is bitter, tasting somewhat of the stone.
Our farmers tell me theirs are all the same;
I think they may have suffered from the drought,
Or from that hail-storm in the early spring.

"Yes, sir! 'tis fifty years in this old house
I've lived; and all these years, day after day,
Have run as even as a ticking clock,
One like another, summer, winter, spring;
And ne'er a day I've failed to have my walk
Down to the Borgo, spite of wind and rain.
While in the valley low the white mist crawls,
I'm up to greet the morning's earliest gleam
Above the hill-tops. After noon I take
An hour's siesta when the birds are still,
And the cicale stop, and, as it were,
All nature falls asleep. As twilight comes,
I take my walk; and, ere the clock strikes ten,
Lie snugly in my bed, and sleep as sound
And dreamless sleep as when I was a boy.

Why should I not? God has been very good,
And given me strength and health! Praise be to Him!

"My life is regular and temperate!
Good wine, sir, never hurts a man; it keeps
The heart and stomach warm—that is, of course,
Unless 'tis taken in excess; but then,
All things are bad, if taken in excess.
I drink my wine more now than once I did;
For as old age comes on I need it more—
But in all things my life is temperate.
I take my cup of coffee when I rise;
I dine at mid-day, and I sup at seven;
I sit upon my loggia, where the vines
Spread their green shadow to keep off the sun,
And there I say my offices and prayers,
And in my well-thumbed breviary read,—
Now listening the birds that chirp and sing;
Now reading of the martyrdom of saints;
Now looking at the peasant in the fields;
Now pondering on the patriarchs of old.
Then there are daily masses—sometimes come

Baptisms, burials, marriages—and so
Life slips along its peaceable routine.

"My people here are generous and kind;
Of all good things they own I have my share,
And I, in turn, do what I can to help,
And smooth away their cares, compose their strifes,
Assuage their sorrows. By kind words alone
One may do much, with the Madonna's aid.
And then, in my small way, I am of use
To cure their ailments: scarce a day goes by
But I must, like a doctor, make my calls,
And see my patients. After fifty years
One must be a physician or a fool.
There's a poor creature now in yonder house
I've spent an hour beside this afternoon,
Holding her hands and whispering words of faith,
And saying what I could to ease her soul.
I know not if she heard me—haply not,
For she is gone almost beyond the reach
Of human language—far, far out alone
On the dim road we all must tread at last.

"Antonio Bucci keeps his lands here well!
An honest, frugal, and industrious man;
And his four daughters,—healthy, handsome girls:
Vittoria is a little wryed, perhaps,
By the Count's admiration—and, in truth,
She is a striking creature; but all that,
You know, is nonsense, and I told her so.
Rosa is married, as you know, and makes
A sturdy wife. She has one little child,
With cheeks like apples. And Regina, too,
And Fanny—both are good and honest girls.
Per Bacco! take them all in all, I think
They're better for Antonio than four boys.
I see them in the early mists of morn
Going a-field; and listen! there they are,
Down in the vineyard, singing, as they tend
Those great white oxen at their evening feed.

"Well, Spitz, we must be going now, or else
Old Nanna 'll scold us both for being late.
Stop barking! Better manners, sir, I say!
He's young, you see; the old one died last spring,

And this one 's over frisky for my age
(You are—you are! you know you are, you scamp!)
But with his foolishness he makes me smile.
As he grows older he'll grow more discreet.
('Tis time to have your supper? So it is!)
And for mine, too, I think—and so, good night!"

So the old curate lifts his hat and smiles,
And shakes his cane at Spitz, and walks away,
A little stiff with age, but strong and hale,
While Spitz whirls round and round before his path,
With volleys of sharp barks, as on they go.
And so Good night! you good old man,—good night!
With your child's heart, despite your eighty years.
I do not ask or care what is your creed—
Your heart is simple, honest, without guile,
Large in its open charity, and prompt
To help your fellow-men,—on such as you,
Whatever be your creed, God's blessing lies.

ZIA NICA.

OLD Zia Nica, she had looked through life—
Its deeps and shoals had sounded—felt the strife
Of storms—sailed round its capes and reefs—and known
The absolute whole of passion's burning zone.
Queen of the osteria there she sat,
Half listening, while around her buzzed its chat;
Her red-rimmed eyes, all bloodshot from carouse,
Half shut, and peering out 'neath shaggy brows;
And now and then a grim sardonic smile
Quivering at some coarse speech across her lips,
As up she sharply glanced, and ceased the while
To drum the table with her finger-tips.
All taste for gracious things was gone; her tongue

Craved the sharp whet of savage words, the zest
Of some lewd speech, some bitter, biting jest,
That like raw brandy for a moment stung.
Thus stern she sat, amid her compeers there,
Over her sunken cheeks her coarse grey hair
Straggling, a wicked sharpness in her look,
Like some spent fury. Now and then she struck
Sharply her clenched hand on the board, until
The glasses rang, and every man was still
To listen, as with voice high, harsh, and shrill,
She shrieked some savage taunt, or jest so lewd,
It seemed to prick the skin and draw the blood ;
And then with coarse laugh opening wide her jaws
(Where, either side the mouth's red-roofed ravine,
Two yellow teeth, like ruined piers, were seen),
She paused, expectant of the fierce applause.
"Bravo, per Bacco ! Zia Nica's shot
Is in the very bull's-eye—is it not?"

If beauty, maidenly reserve, and grace,
Once, as they say, in earlier, happier hours,
Grassed softly over this volcano's vent,

The time has long gone by of grass or flowers;
Ay, and the passionate and flaming days,
They, too, have passed, and all their fury spent,
And left but ashes, scoriæ, blasted stones,
Cast forth by passion, the dead wreck of sin.
Yet impotent, low growls, and rumbling moans,
And sharp convulsive throes, still stir within;
Still the old crater, burnt out at its heart,
At times a savage tongue of flame will dart;
And Zio Tonio trembles even now,
Despite his coward smile, so faint and grim—
Trembles, as down she shuts her dinted brow,
And her eyes, closing, take slow aim at him.

And yet not wholly vanished is all grace;
One vein of love runs like a singing stream
Through all this scoriæ; and across her face,
Praise but her grandchild, shoots a sudden gleam,
As she strokes down his curled and tangled hair.
Touch him for harm,—the tiger from her lair
Is not more swift to spring, more wild to scream,
More fierce with hand and tongue to rend and tear.
Come, Zia Nica, then, a brimming glass!

Nay, sit not thus, your hands upon your knees,
But drain its red blood down unto the lees.
Yours is no heart to strike to an "alas";—
Up! while the mandoline and thrummed guitar
Ring through the osteria's vaulted wall,
And all our glasses jar and voices call—
Hark to the echoes of the days afar!
Hands on your broad hips,—shuffle down the floor
A tottering salterello,—pipe once more
That old cracked voice,—and while the noisy jar
Of Passatello stops, and we who quaff
The rich red wine of Tonio's choicest bin,
Strike down our tumblers,—shriek out shrill and long
The quavering fragment of that wicked song,
And let us hear your wild defiant laugh
Closing the final strophe of its sin.
Then shall the black vault echo to the din,
The benches leap, the lumbering tables spring,
The brass lucerna's rattling pendants swing,
The hanging lamp in quivering circles shake,
And o'er the ceiling whirl its gleaming ring,
Ay, and the framed Madonna, shuddering, quake.

Up, Zia Nica! hear you not the strain?
Once you could dance. Old Tonio, stand aside.
Push back the benches! make the circle wide!
The music rouses the old strength again.
Ay! when this Tonio took her for his bride,
Was there, of all the maids on hill or plain,
One that with this fierce mænad could compare?
More firm of waist, with such black eyes and hair?

Stand back! there's danger in her eyes; for lo!
Upstarting with a sharp shriek from her seat,
With arms flung wide, and heavy shuffling feet,
Around the cleared space see her circling go.
Her trembling hands now twitching at her gown,
Now snapped aloft in air,—till, flushed with heat,
All reeking, panting, shaking, in her seat,
With open mouth, she drops, exhausted, down,
Crying—"Old Zia Nica's not dead yet!"
To Zia Nica, then, your glasses drain!
And let the low room echo to the cry—
Eviva! and eviva! and again
Eviva!—may our Zia never die!

L'ABBATE.

WERE it not for that singular smell
  That seems to the genus priest to belong,
Where snuff and incense are mingled well
  With a natural odour quite as strong :
Were it not for those little ways
  Of clasped and deprecating hands ;
And of raising and lowering his eyes always
  As if he only waited commands—

Little there is in him of the priest,
  With only the slightest touch of cant,
With a simple, guileless heart in his breast,
  And a mind as honest as ignorant.

Half a child and half a man,
  Ripe in the Fathers and green in thought,
In his little circle of half a span
  He thinks he thinks what he was taught.

His duty he does to the scruple's weight;
  Recites his prayers, and mumbles his mass,
And without his litanies, early and late,
  Never permits a day to pass.
Look at him there in the garden-plots
  Repeating his office, as to and fro
He paces around the orange-pots,
  Looking about while his quick lips go.

His simple pleasure in simple things,
  His willing spirit that never tires,
His trivial jokes and wonderings,
  His peaceful temper that never fires,
His joy over trifles of every day,
  The feeble poems he loves to quote,—
Are just like a child, with his heart in his play,
  While his duty and lessons are drill and rote.

What life means he does not think ;
  Reason and thought he has been told
Only lead to a perilous brink,
  Away from Christ and the Church's fold.
Therefore he humbly and blindly obeys ;
  Does what he's ordered and reasons not ;
Performs his prayers, and thinks he prays,
  And asks not how, or why, or what.

Happy in this, why stir his mind,
  Stagnant in thought although it be?
Leave him alone—he is gentle and kind,
  And blest with a child's simplicity.
Thinking would only give him unrest,
  Struggle, and toil, and inward strain ;
His heart is right in his thoughtless breast,
  Why should one wish to torment his brain?

Yet out of pastime one evil day
  I unfolded to him Pythagoras' plan—
How step by step the soul made its way
  From sea-anemone up to man,—

How onward to higher grades it went,
  If its human life had been fair and pure ;
Or if not, to the lower scale was sent,
  Again to ascend to man, and endure.

And so the soul had gleams of the past,
  And felt in itself dim sympathies
With nature, that ended in us at last,
  And each of whose forms within us lies.
He smiled at first, and then by degrees
  Grew silent and sad, and confessed 'twas true,
But with spirit so pained and ill at ease,
  That my foolish work I strove to undo.

This thinking's the spawn of Satan, I said,
  That tempts us into the sea of doubt ;
And Satan has endless snares to spread,
  If once with our reason we venture out.
Here you are in your Church like a port,
  Anchored secure, where never a gale
Can break your moorings,—nor even in sport
  Should you weigh your anchor or spread your sail.

So I got him back to his anchor again,
  And there in the stagnant harbour he lies;
And he looks upon me with a sense of pain
  As a wild freebooter; for to his eyes
Free thinking, free sailing seems to be,
  A sort of a godless, dangerous thing,
Like a pirate's life on a stormy sea—
  And sure at the last damnation to bring.

N I N A.

[*Dedicated to M. E. B.*]

How bright, how glad, how gay,
  To thee, O Nina, dear!
Day after day slipped smooth away,
  Through childhood's simple joy and simple fear.
    Strained by no adverse force,
Life, like a clear and placid stream
  In some delightful clime,
Bearing the sky within it like a dream,
  And all the fair reflected shapes of time,
    Flowed on its gentle course!
How many a time, oppressed with gloom,
While sitting in my lonely room,

And toiling at my task,
Neglected, humble, wan with care,
Aspiring, hoping, though I did not dare
Fate's laurelled prize to ask,
Have I been gladdened by that voice of thine,
Singing, perhaps, some trivial song of mine,
And listened, and looked up, and felt a thrill
Come o'er my heart—as over waters still
A light breeze flutters—and almost forgot,
Hearing that happy voice, my wretched lot.

Years went; the round and rosy face
Grew fairer, paler; and as Childhood went,
Came Maidenhood's more tender grace
And thoughtful sentiment:
And when the first soft airs of Spring
Wooed the flowers forth, and with a subtle fire
Stirred in the human heart a vague desire
For what life cannot bring,
Often I watched you moving to and fro
The alleys of the garden-plot below,
Your white gown 'mid the roses fluttering;

And now you paused to train some wandering spray
    With almost a caress,
And now you plucked some last year's leaf away
    That marred its perfectness;
Or where the lilies of the valley grew,
Like them as modest, sweet, and pale of hue,
You bent to breathe their odour, or to give—
Almost it seemed as if they must receive
From you a sweeter odour than they knew.

Sometimes, as lingering there you walked along,
Humming half consciously some little song,
You paused, looked up, and saw me, mute and still,
Gazing upon you from my window-sill;
And with a voice, so glad and clear,
It rang like music on my ear—
You cried, "Antonio! look, Antonio, dear!"
Ah, happy memories!
They bring the burning tears into my eyes.
Oh, speak again, and say, "Antonio, dear!"
Ah, vanished voice! call to me once again!

Never! ah, never! in this world of pain,
No tone like thine my heart will ever thrill.

Oft when the spring its perfumed violets strewed
Along the greensward, 'neath the ilex wood
I strolled with you, how many an afternoon,
In the perfection of the early June—
Not owning to myself, as there we roved,
Not knowing, truly knowing, that I loved;
And all the while your pure young thought
So deeply in my inmost being wrought,
That it became a happy part of me—
And as it were a sweet necessity—
From which I wanted never to be free.

Yet never spoke I of my love; so slow,
  So gently in my heart it grew,
That when it fully came I scarcely know—
  Not bursting into rapture strange and new,
Splendour and perfume on the air to pour,
That from the sense was hidden in the bud
    A little hour before;

But slowly rising, like a tide to brim
  My being, widening ever more and more,
And deepening all my central life with dim
  Unconscious fulness, till its joy ran o'er.
    Then, when I knew at last,
    How very dear thou wast,
I dared not trust my tongue to ease the load
  Of love that lay upon my heart,
  But lonely, silent, and apart,
Of you I dreamed—for you I hourly prayed—
Glad of my secret love, but how afraid!

'Twas but a child's affection that you bore
For me—a placid feeling—nothing more.
Across your heart, so gentle and serene,
The burning thrill of love had never been;
And childhood scarce had given place
To maidenhood's more subtle grace,
  When Death, who darkly walks along
  Amid the gentle and the strong,
When least we fear to see his face,
Paused, gazed at you, and took you for his own,

And all the joy from out my life had flown--
  And I was left of all bereft,
    Too utterly alone.

    Will earth again renew
That simple love for me?—ah, no!
Spring comes again—again the roses blow—
    But you—ah, me!—not you!
  Oh, Nina! in your grassy grave
    I buried what can never grow again;
  Life but one perfect joy can have—
    That in thy grave is lain!

GIULIETTA.

[*Dedicated to G. W. C.*]

AH, how still the moonbeams lie
 On the dreaming meadows!
How the fire-flies silently
 Lighten through the shadows!
All the cypress avenue
Waves its tops against the blue,
As the wind slides whispering through—
  He is late in coming!

There's the nightingale again!
 He alone is waking;
Is it joy or is it pain
 That his heart is breaking?

Bliss intense or pain divine?
Both of them, oh Love, are thine!
And this heart, this heart of mine,
With them both is thrilling.

From the deep dark orange-grove
Odorous airs are streaming,
Till my thoughts are faint with love—
Faint with blissful dreaming.
Through the slopes of dewy dells
Crickets shake their tiny bells,
And the sky's deep bosom swells
With an infinite yearning.

On my heart the silent weight
Of this beauty presses;
Midnight, like a solemn Fate,
Saddens while it blesses.
All alone I cannot bear
This still night and odorous air;
Dearest, come, its bliss to share,
Or I die with longing.

I have listened at the doors,
  All are calmly sleeping;
I alone for hours and hours
  In the dark am weeping.
Only weeping can express
The mysterious deep excess
Of my very happiness,
    Therefore I am weeping.

Like a fountain running o'er
  With its too great fulness,
Like a lightning-shivered shower
  For the fierce noon's coolness,
Like an over-blossomed tree,
That the breeze shakes tenderly,
Love's too much falls off from me
    In these tears of gladness.

Ah, beloved! there you are!
  I once more am near you;
Walk not on the gravel there,
  Somebody may hear you.

Step upon the noiseless grass;
Oh ! if they should hear you pass
We are lost, alas ! alas !
    We are lost for ever!

Look ! the laurels in the light
    Seem with eyes to glisten ;
All things peep and peer—and night
    Holds its breath to listen.
Deeper in the shadow move,
For the moon looks out above,
I am coming to you, love,
  In a moment coming.

IN THE RAIN.

I STAND in the cold grey weather,
  In the white and silvery rain;
The great trees huddle together,
  And sway with the windy strain.
I dream of the purple glory
  Of the roseate mountain-height,
And the sweet-to-remember story
  Of a distant and dear delight.

The rain keeps constantly raining,
  And the sky is cold and grey,
And the wind in the trees keeps complaining,
  That summer has passed away;—

But the grey and the cold are haunted
  By a beauty akin to pain,—
By the sense of a something wanted,
  That never will come again.

THE LILAC.

THE lilac-bush is in blossom,
  It hath the balmy smell
Of that dear delicious summer,
  Of love's first miracle.
I feel, as I breathe its fragrance,
  The old enchanting pain,
The sweet insatiate longing,
  Thrill through my heart and brain.

Oh youth ! youth ! youth ! where are you ?
  I call, but you come no more !
I weep, but afar you mock me !
  And you laugh when I implore !

Yet you hide within the lilac,
  With an odour you shoot me through,
And a whiff of the old you fling me
  That is better than all the new.

How proudly we struggled to leave you,
  When you implored us to stay!
How bitterly grieve to regain you
  When once you have fled away.
Too late, too late, we love you,
  And long for your laugh of surprise,
And we only truly can see you
  With manhood's tears in our eyes.

You flung your arms around me
  And pelted me with flowers;
You clung to me as we wandered
  Among those lilac bowers.
You kissed me, half laughing, half crying,
  Beseeching me to remain,
But impatient I shook you from me—
  And you never will come again.

Your lilacs are ever blooming
  In happy gardens of play,
But they love you not who have you,
  And fain would they flee away.
They long for the fields of freedom
  Where the fruit of ambition grows,
And for manhood's heights, that are lifted
  Against a sky of rose.

THE GAUCHO.

OVER the lonely, desolate Pampas,
  A sinewy horse my flying throne,
Coiled at my saddle-bow the lasso,
  In my belt a knife that reaches the bone.
I am the Gaucho,—riding, hiding,
  Whirling the bolas, wielding the knife,
Over the prairies of Buenos Ayres,
Let him who would take me look out for his life!

Ne'er a tide but the fleeting seasons
  Sweeps o'er the inland sea of grass;
Roaring herds, like clouds of thunder,
  Over its lonely levels pass.

Jaguars yell; and, striding, hiding,
  Ostriches rush—for they fear the knife—
Over the prairies of Buenos Ayres,
Let him who pursues me look out for his life!

With my tongues of cows and gourd of yerba,
  And the cigaritos smoke on my hearth,
I laugh at your houses; my saddle 's my pillow,
  My chamber a thousand miles of earth.
With the stars above me gliding, hiding,
  I lie at ease, as I grasp my knife.
On the wide prairies of Buenos Ayres,
Let him who awakes me look out for his life!

Look! in the distance a cloud is rising;
  In with the spur! fling loose the rein!
Sharp sings the lasso's loop as it whizzes,—
  And the bellowing bull drops on the plain.
Out from my saddle sliding, gliding,
  Deep in his throat my flashing knife.
O'er the wide prairies of Buenos Ayres,
Let him who pursues me look out for his life!

Keep your dragoons at home—I warn you!
  For the Gaucho writes his laws in blood;
The bolas are ready; coiled is the lasso;
  And this white dust can be red mud.
You for the crows, and, riding, riding,
  I for the Andes with my knife.
Over the prairies of Buenos Ayres,
Let him who would take me look out for his life!

SPRING.

Doves on the sunny eaves are cooing,
  The chip-bird trills from the apple-tree,
Blossoms are bursting, and leaves renewing,
  And the crocus darts up, the Spring to see.

Spring has come with a smile of blessing,
  Kissing the earth with her soft warm breath
Till it blushes in flowers at her gentle caressing,
  And wakes from the winter's dream of death.

Spring has come! the rills as they glisten
  Sing to the pebbles and greening grass,

Under the sward the violets listen,
  And dream of the sky as they hear her pass.

Coyest of roses feel her coming,
  Swelling their buds with a promise to her,
And the wild bee hears her, around them humming,
  And booms about with a joyous stir.

Oaks, that the bark of a century covers,
  Feel ye the spell as ye groan and sigh?
Say, does the spirit that round you hovers
  Whisper of youth and love gone by?

Windows are open; the pensive maiden
  Leans o'er the sill with a wistful sigh,—
Her heart with tender longings o'erladen,
  And a happy sadness she knows not why.

For we and the trees are brothers in nature;
  We feel in our veins the season's thrill,
In hopes, that reach to a higher stature,
  In blind dim longings beyond our will.

Whence dost thou come, oh joyous spirit?
From realms beyond this human ken,
To paint with beauty the earth we inherit,
And soften to love the hearts of men?

Dear angel! that blowest with breath of gladness
The trump to waken the year in its grave,
Shall we not hear after death's deep sadness
A voice as tender to gladden and save?

Dost thou not sing a constant promise,
That joy shall follow that other voice,—
That nothing of good shall be taken from us,
But all who hear it shall rise to rejoice?

A U T U M N.

[*Dedicated to J. R. L.*]

THESE Autumn winds are growing chill,
They wander wailing o'er the hill,
And at the close-shut window cry
That summer opened lovingly;
But we can let them in no more,
And all the eve my heart is sore—
My heart is sore, I know not why.
    They seem to say,
    The summer day
    Has past away,
And life goes with it silently.

Still o'er the mountain's darkening bar
We watch the new-born evening star,
That throbs and quivers in the sea
Of amber light—and musingly
We let our shaping fancy play
With those soft clouds of pearly grey,
That float along the silvery sky.
Ah woe! ah woe!
We all must go,
The chill winds blow,
And summer 's gone like a passing sigh.

These Autumn morns when we may stray
Through chestnut woods, where glancing play
The checkered light and shadow thrown
O'er trunk, and grass, and mossy stone,
And lie beneath some spreading tree
And feel our own felicity,
How sweet if they would never fly—
But no! ah no!
'Tis never so!
All good things go,
And thought pursues them with a sigh.

All day the woods are redolent
And saddened with the steamy scent
The dewy rotting leaves exhale
That heap the hollows in the vale;
Then through the bonfire's quivering gas
The landscape shakes as it would pass,
And all is sad, we know not why;—
All seems to say
The summer day
Is past away,
Why linger ye to say Good-bye?

No more the fierce cicala shrills,
Only the hearthstone-cricket trills,—
The hemp-stalks pile their bleaching bones
In pyramids of skeletons,
Or clacking cradles break them where
The peasant shakes their silvery hair,
And flings them on the grass to dry.
The summer's flown,
The leaves are strewn,
And we alone
Are lingering here to say Good-bye.

The cyclamen, alive with fears,
Smoothes trembling back its harelike ears;
The frost-touched creepers bleeding fall,
And drip in crimson o'er the wall;
The rusted chestnuts shivering spill
Their bursting spine-burrs on the hill;
The day is short, soon comes the night,
    And damp and chill
    Along the hill
    The dews distil
Under the harvest-moon's great light.

Louder at eve the river roars;
The fringed acacia paves with showers
Of golden leaves our summer path,
And all the world about us hath
A feel of sorrow—we must go;
Alas! I would not have it so,
But all things vanish from us here,
    And still we sigh,
    Ah why, ah why,
    So swiftly fly,
Ye days that were so glad and dear?

'Tis lovely still; but yet a sense
Of sadness and impermanence
Disturbs me—and this flushing grace
That mantles over Autumn's face
Is but the hectic hue, beneath
Whose beauty steals the thought of death,—
And this it is that makes us sigh.
    Ah! bitter word
    Too often heard,
    What thoughts are stirred
Whene'er we whisper thee—Good-bye!

Death walks along my shrouded thought;
I feel him though I see him not:
His step is on the joys that grew
And waved this lovely summer through.
I fear, for life is all too fair,
And trembling ask, Ah! when? and where?
And this it is that makes me sigh;
    Too sweet to last,
    Ah! golden past
    That fled so fast,
No future owns such witchery.

AN ENGLISH HUSBAND TO HIS ITALIAN WIFE.

WHAT a constant jealousy gnaws your heart!
 It tires me out; day after day
Some little worry from nothing you start—
 Something's hidden in what I say,
Something's hidden in what I do;
 That heart of yours is never still,
It cannot be sure that I am true,
 But spies and pries about for ill.

Frankly I speak the whole of my mind
 Once for all—let it serve or not:
I am not one of that showy kind,
 Fair outside with an inward rot.

I love you! will not that suffice?
  No! I must say it again and again,
And embroider it over with flatteries,
  Or all I have said and done is vain.

Trust me! trust my simple love!
  If you suspect me, that love will die.
I cannot bear to be forced to prove
  Every moment its honesty.
Ah! you say, I'm so still and cold!
  Well! I cannot be other than what I am;
I cannot squander my lump of gold
  As I could a little tinsel sham.

You your jewels must always wear;
  What is their use if they are not shown?
I keep mine with a miser's care,
  And love to count them over alone.
I cannot abide that the world should observe.
  What it thinks is nothing to me;
I was born with a sense of reserve
  That is shocked by love's publicity.

You have a richer heart, if you will,
That scatters about its wide largess;
Your love a keeping like mine would kill,—
All that you feel you must express.
Your love seeks for the light and sun,
And gives its perfume to every breeze;
The bees get its honey—every one—
Its beauty whoever passes sees.

Mine, like a well, is still and deep:
Cold, you say it is, like a well;
But though like a brook it will not leap
And joy for ever one tale to tell,
It still is real; and when the year
Hath silenced the brook with its shallow laugh
The well's cool waters will still be clear,
Where those who trusted may surely quaff.

I cannot, like Sarto, publish your face
In every Madonna, Sibyl, and Saint,
Or praise to the world your beauty and grace
In a thousand sonnets sweet and faint.

But this is the head's work more than the heart's:
  Skill and genius they show, no doubt;
But the painter and poet may give to their Arts
  What they leave their lady, perhaps, without.

Trust me, dear, with your eyes so black
  And full of passion,—these eyes of blue,
Though your excess of expression they lack,
  Are not the less sincere and true.
I cannot fondle you every hour
  With many a pretty and gallant phrase,
Rain out my love as a cloud its shower,—
But trust me, and leave me my English ways.

IN THE MOONLIGHT.

We sat in the perfect moonlight;
  The stars were dim and rare,
And above us the elm-trees rustled
  In the waves of the cool night-air.

From the olives and vineyard near us
  The kiou-owl plaintively cried,
And away o'er the misty hollows
  Its mate with a wail replied.

The peasant sang in the distance,
  The watchdog barked at the star,

And the clack of the cradles beating the hemp
   Came faint from the farms afar.

We talked of the times of our childhood,
   Of the days for ever flown,
Of their games and their jests and their sorrows,
   And the playmates we had known;

And then there came o'er us a silence,
   While the cypresses sighed overhead,—
And dreaming we sat and listened
   To the voices of the dead.

NEMESIS.

[Dedicated to E. B. H.]

OPPRESSED by pain, by grief subdued,
I closed at night my weary eyes,
When, in the dubious twilight dim
Betwixt reality and dream,
The awful shape of Nemesis—
The absolute—before me stood.

Her hands within her robes involved,
And folded square upon her breast,
Immovable, in perfect rest,
From sight of human eyes concealed
The dread decree of Fate she held,
By time and death to be resolved.

Severe was she in mood and mien,
Like one who never saw surprise;
Who, deaf alike to love or hate,
Or joy or fear, impassionate
Decreed the doom—decreed the prize—
Inexorable, yet serene.

"Oh! what hast thou for me in store
This side the shadow of the tomb?
Pronounce!" I cried, "or what shall be
The stern decree of destiny
When life and death alike are o'er?"

"Time is of destiny the womb,"
She answered. "Seek not to explore
What the eternal powers above
Conceal, in pity and in love,
Behind the Future's darkened door.

"Content within the present live!
Do the great duty of to-day!
Minute by minute the gods give,

Each unto each for man to lay—
Not to be scorned—nor thrown away.

"With love and justice build them close
By strenuous act and earnest will!
Nor let your wandering wishes loose
To anxious hopes or fears of ill—
So will you best time's task fulfil!

"Pile not with vain regrets the grave
Of the irrevocable past!
Seize opportunity—enslave
The living moments while they last!
For Fortune meets half-way the brave."

She ceased; and starting from my sleep,
I heard the roaring thunder, thrown
Far down from mountain steep to steep,
And dying in a distant groan,—
And waking, found myself alone.

BLACK EYES.

THOSE black eyes I once so praised,
  Now are hard and sharp and cold;
Where's the love that through them blazed?
  Where's the tenderness of old?
All is gone—how utterly—
  From its stem the flower has dropped.
Ah! how ugly Life can be
  After Love from it is lopped!

Do we hate each other now,
  While we call each other dear?
On that faultless mouth and brow
  To the world does change appear?

No! your smile is just as sweet,
  Just as fair your outward grace;
But I look in vain to greet
  The dear ghost behind the face.

That is gone! I look on you
  As a corpse from which has fled
All that once I loved and knew,
  All that once I thought to wed.
'Tis not your fault, 'tis not mine;
  Yet I still recall a dream
Of a joy almost divine—
  'Twas an image in a stream.

Nothing can be sour and sharp
  As a love that has decayed—
On the loose strings of the harp
  Only discord can be made.
Cold this common friendship seems
  After love's auroral glow;
On the broken stem of dreams
  Only disappointments grow.

Do I hate you? No! Not hate?
Hate 's a word far too intense,
Too alive, to speak a state
Of supreme indifference.
Once, behind your eyes I thought
Worlds of love and life to see;
Now I see behind them nought
But a soulless vacancy.

Out and out I know you now;
There's no issue of your heart
Where my soul with you may go
To a beauty all apart,
Where the world can never come.
'Tis a little narrow place—
Friendship there might find a home;
Love would die—for want of space.

So we live! The world still says,
"What expression in her eyes!
What sweet manners—graceful ways!"
How it would the world surprise

If I said, "This woman's soul
  Made for love you think, but try;
Plunge therein—how clear and shoal!—
  You might drown there—so can't I?"

THE SAD COUNTRY.

THERE is a sad, sad country,
  Where often I go to see
A little child that for all my love
  Will never come back to me.

There smiles he serenely on me
  With a look that makes me cry;
And he prattling runs beside me
  Till I wish that I could die.

That country is dim and dreary,
  Yet I cannot keep away,

Though the shadows there are heavy and dark,
  And the sunlight sadder than they.

And there, in a ruined garden,
  Which once was gay with flowers,
I sit by a broken fountain,
  And weep and pray for hours.

CASTEL GANDOLFO.

[*Dedicated to L. C.*]

THE fountain on the moonlight plays,
  And old Castello's turrets rise
  Darkly against the silvery skies,
And voices laugh along the ways.

The moonlight sleeps upon the square;
  And from the castellated town
  The sharp dark blocks of shadow thrown
Lie cut out in the whiteness there.

Among the trees the luccioli
  Show fitfully their wandering light,

And far away across the night
The owl prolongs his dreary cry.

How still! how exquisitely still!
No sound disturbs the silentness
Save the untiring cricket's stress,
And the continuous fountain's spill.

The weeds along the old grey wall
Hang moveless, casting spots of shade;
And all is beautified, and made
More perfect where the moonbeams fall.

What magic light that thus can hide
The ravages of time, and grace
The commonest and meanest place,
And veil the earth as 'twere a bride!

On such a night Diana kissed
Endymion's brow the while he slept,
As noiselessly to him she crept
Enshrouded in a silver mist.

Oh ! pass not, perfect night, from us,
  But stay with us and crown our love !
  Sing, from the shadowy ilex grove—
Sing, nightingale, for ever thus !

AT PEACE.

'Tis twilight! the murmurous voices
Of maidens that stroll with their lovers
Beneath the dark ilex's shadows
    Come faint to my ear.

No cloud in the soft azure heaven
Is floating—the moon in its fulness
Looks down with a mild face of pity,
    And night holds its breath.

Innumerous under the grasses
The grilli are ceaselessly chirping,

Above them the luccioli lighten,
 And all is at peace !

At peace ! ay, the peace of the desert !
The silence, the deep desolation,
That comes when the blast has swept o'er us
 And buried our hopes.

At peace ! when the music that thrilled us,
The hand that its harmonies wakened,
The voice that was soul to the singing,
 Alike are at rest !

At peace ! ay, the peace of the ocean,
When past is the storm where we foundered,
And morning looks o'er the blank waters,
 And hears but their moan !

WOGGINS.

SINGING little artless snatches,
  Words and music all her own,
While her dolls she tends and dresses,
  By herself, but not alone,
Round from room to room she wanders,
  Through the hall, and up the stairs,
And her sunny buoyant spirit
  Knows but trivial shades and cares.

Now upon the stair she's singing;
  Now, in corners of the rooms,
Self-involved, her little household
  Patronising she assumes.

What a teeming world of fiction
  Out of nothing she creates!
Fancy, childhood's gentle fairy,
  With her wand upon her waits.

Little scraps of worthless paper,
  Scribbled o'er with crooked lines,
She interprets into landscapes
  Where an endless sunlight shines.
Conversations wise and serious
  With her painted dolls she holds;
And the good ones she caresses,
  And the naughty ones she scolds.

Now she brings her book of pictures,
  And with large and wondering eyes,
On my knee she sits and listens
  With a smile of young surprise,
While I tell the same old stories
  I have told her o'er and o'er
Scores of times, yet when I finish,
  With a shout she cries, "Tell more!"

Knowledge, that the mind encumbers,
  Cares, that after-years harass,
Are to her but misty sun-showers,
  Rainbow traps that come and pass.
All the world is as a plaything—
  When it wearies, thrown away,
As from new to new she ranges
  In the imagination's play.

Wisdom such as thine I covet,
  Happy childhood! Work and toil,
Plans that never reach enjoyment,
  But the present's beauty spoil,
Are not made for thee; contented
  With the present, from each day
But its juice of joy thou pressest,
  Fling'st the bitter rind away.

Not till man through toil and labour
  Onward pass to joyous ease,
Not till knowing rhyme with loving,
  Nature will give up its keys.

All is shut to poet, artist,
  Till he be a child again;
And in play shall be created
  What was never born of pain.

UNDER THE CYPRESSES.

Here I stand in the cypress lane;
  I see the light in her window shine;
Ah, God! can this love be all in vain,
  And shall she never be mine?

There stays her shadow against the walls;
  There moves on the ceiling to and fro:
She does not think of the heart that calls
  So loud in the dark below.

Why should she think of a fool like me,
  Though I'd give my life to save her a pain?

The stars might as well look down to see
  The fire-flies in the lane.

I am too low for her to love;
  And I would not give her the pain to say
That a love like mine could only prove
  A shadow upon her way.

So I stand in the cypress shade and weep—
  I weep, for my heart is sick with love;
And I pray for strength my vow to keep,
  As I gaze on the sky above.

Is it wrong to gaze at her window-sill,
  Where she sits like an angel in a shrine,
While my heart cries out, despite my will,
  "Ah, heaven! were she but mine?"

Heart of mine, I could tear you out!
  Am I so weak and faint of will
That the fair dear serpent coiled about
  My purpose I cannot kill?

Where is my vaunted manhood fled?
  Come, my pride—my pride, come back!
Serve me and prompt me a while, instead
  Of all I so sadly lack!

Vain! ah, vain! all day and night
  One thought, like a ghost, I cannot lay,
Ranges my life and haunts my sight,
  And never will pass away.

It mocks me and beckons at my work,
  It lures me away from joy and ease;
Where shall I flee that it does not lurk,
  This shadow no hand can seize?

Give me something to meet and grasp!
  I faint with fighting this thing of air!
I die despairing in its clasp!
  Its presence I cannot bear!

Oh, give me strength, my God, to endure!
  Let me not writhe to death in the grass!

Send me, ye stars, from your chambers pure,
  Some ease, as ye coldly pass!

Look at this poor mad wretch that lies
  Beating his brain that is all afire!
Pity him here as he grovelling dies
  In the flames of his vain desire!

TO BIANCA.

"Tu ne quæsieris, scire nefas."

CEASE to peer into the future, nor torture yourself with
care
Of fancied delights or troubles that never may fall to
your share!
The present alone is ours; in that let us live content,
Enjoying the daily blessings the gods for the moment
have lent.

And cease to torment your spirit with that which has
passed away,
The love that has vanished, the passion, the folly that
led you astray;

Not hoping too much, not regretting—for what is more
vain than regret?—
And, never the gladness forgetting, the pain and the
sorrow forget.

Take, oh Bianca, the beauty and joy of the world to thy
heart!
For the power to enjoy is not only a blessing,—'tis also
an art.
And be glad for the gifts that are granted, nor envy
what cannot be thine;
For the life, that with Fate is in balance, is peaceful,
and, so far, divine.

THE PADRE AND THE NOVICE.

[*Dedicated to R. L.*]

I.

Do you hear, Lorenzo? I say these wishes and vague desires
Will all of them pass away, though now they seem so bright;
They are will-o'-the-wisps that breed uncertain treacherous fires:
No real lamps that lead the traveller through the night.

II.

My youth has gone like a song. You heed not an old man's words.
Yet once, like you, I was young. Alas! I know it all;

And often my memory smites my thoughts, and awakens chords
Of far and dim delights, that I tremble as I recall.

III.

I loved! Ah! yes, I loved with a love that maddened my mind—
With a passion that reason reproved—I loved, as I pray to God
You never may love, my boy; and the storm came down, and the wind,
And my hope was crushed, and my joy—as you crush these flowers in the sod.

IV.

I awoke—as a man may wake from a wild and feverish dream—
Useless and helpless—a wreck,—with scarcely the wish or power
On the spars of life to drift,—and a fierce regret that the stream,
Sweeping to death so swift, had flung me aside for an hour.

V.

Slowly the world came back; but oh! how changed
and dear!
The serpent was on its track—my spirit was bitter and
dark.
I rushed to battle;—Death passed me, shaking his
sword and spear,
And, scornful, aside he cast me, making the happy his
mark.

VI.

But the savage hate of life died down like a fading
flame;
And weary and worn with strife, and broken and spent
with care,—
With a spirit inly stirred, to the convent grate I came,
And God in His mercy heard,—and peace returned with
prayer.

VII.

There is peace, that nothing taints, in the life that to
God is given—
To Christ, and the holy saints—that minister unto
man;

For the world is a snare and a lure that leads us away
from heaven,
And Love is a demon impure, that tears us whenever it
can.

VIII.

Ah ! flee from the coils it spreads. Oh yield not unto
its snare !
Gilded at first its threads, in torture at last they end ;
And Love, like the Sphinx of old, with its bosom and
face so fair,
Hath arms of the tiger to hold, and claws of the tiger to
rend.

IX.

Look not back—be advised—on the path you have
chosen so well.
The Church is the fold of Christ : the world is the
devil's den.
Hark ! 'tis the Angelus, ringing afar from the convent
bell—
Ave Maria sanctissima, ora pro nobis.—Amen.

UNDER A CLOUD.

Ah me! I'm so ill and weary,
  I wish I could only die!
For here all alone and dreary,
  As hour after hour I lie,
I think it all over and over,
  And see no issue of peace;
No way the lost joy to recover,
  If death do not give me release.

I know not what change may come after,
  But *that* I take upon trust;
Perhaps no more weeping nor laughter—
  Only a handful of dust.

Perhaps a glory and gladness
  We never have dreamt of here,
Where love has no shadow of sadness,
  And joy has no shudder of fear.

At least I shall no more sorrow,
  And suffer such helpless pain,
With no hope for the coming morrow,
  No hope to behold him again.
And that terrible longing and craving
  Again in his arms to be,
Will cease in my heart to be raving
  And tearing me inwardly.

But then, perhaps, I shall lose him—
  And here, if I strive and stay,
Since God is so good, if one sues Him,
  Perhaps he will open a way—
Some way through this tangle of anguish
  To a joy beyond our sight,
Nor leave as to linger and languish,
  Like creatures lost in the night.

Here, as I lie, I go over
  The dear departed days,
When my love I began to discover,
  Till my thoughts are all in a craze;
And the vines on the sunny terrace,
  Through the windows again I see;
And the room with the quaint old arras,
  Where he whispered his love to me.

But what is the use of thinking?
  'Tis all like a sleepless pain,
That keeps tramping, tramping, and clinking
  In the treadmill of my brain.
'Tis like hearing the music for ever
  Going on to the dancers' tread,
While I'm fainting and dying with fever,
  And helpless to lift my head.

I am getting so old with fretting,
  Perhaps he will love me no more;
And I sometimes fear his forgetting,
  And this makes my heart so sore.

And before the stone that is lying
  Across my path is removed,
Who knows but that he may be dying,
  To make it vain that we loved.

Oh Nannie, you soon will be strewing
  The flowers on the bed where I lie!
Last week I thought I was going!
  But oh, 'tis so hard to die!
Life beat in my bosom so slowly,
  Though a fever was in my brain—
And everything went from me wholly,
  Save a numb, dull sense of pain.

In body and mind I seemed doubled;
  And one was so tired and weak,
And the other was dead and untroubled—
  Too dead to feel or to speak.
And the tired body kept praying,
  "Make me, too, cold and numb."
"Let me sleep, let me sleep," it kept saying—
  But sleep would never come.

Oh God! that it all were over,
For life is not worth its cost;
And I know I can never recover
The joy and the peace that are lost.
Death only can break the fetter,
Death only can set things straight;
And death, after all, is better
Than a lifelong struggle with fate.

Tell George he must try and forgive me,
For my struggle, though vain, was sore;
And beg him in quiet to leave me,
And scold and reproach me no more.
I was weak—but 'tis useless to chide me,
Let him leave me alone to God;
And bury my sins beside me,
When he lays me under the sod.

THE SHADY LANE.

I WAITED for him in the shady lane,
  For I knew he would pass there late at night;
And that leaf-strewn wood I swore to stain
  With his blood or mine, for I hated his sight.
There I waited and listened alone,
  With a tumult of rage in my heart and brain;
And I swore to myself the deed should be done
  To-night, as he passed the lane.

Was I not right? He had stolen her heart—
  My heart, that more than my life was dear;
Had poisoned her mind with his treacherous art,
  And his vile love breathed in her ear.

He, the contemptible trivial fool,
  With never a scruple or doubt or fear
Of his exquisite self—to make her the tool
  Of his flatteries insincere!

Why did she blush as she heard him speak,
  Flushing all over as red as a rose
When he touched her hand? and tremble, as weak
  As a reed when a light wind blows.
What was there, I say, in that empty face,
  In that empty head, and emptier heart,
That gave him the power her name to disgrace,
  And my darling from me to part?

I knew his step, as gaily he came,
  Swinging his stick as he strode along—
Hate lightened along my nerves like flame,
  I was mad to hear him singing *that* song.
Before him I leaped with a single bound,
  Face to face in the pale moonlight—
"No words," I cried; "blows, blows, you hound;
  One of us two must die to-night."

Aghast he stood, but not with fear,
  Most with the suddenness of the thing—
As one when the sky is bright and clear
  Starts at the lightning's sudden sting.
"You!" he cried. "Back; let me pass!
  Back, I say; are you drunk or mad?"
"Both," I cried. "You have ruined the lass;
  And your blood shall answer, my lad."

We fought together there in the shade,
  As a madman and his keeper fight;
He for his life, that love had made
  So sweet, and I for his death, that night.
That love!—a fire was in my brain,
  The strength of a fiend was in my hand,
And at last he dropped in the shady lane,
  And his blood oozed out on the sand.

"My life! don't murder me," he said,
  As I clenched him there—when suddenly
The struggling body lay heavy and dead,
  And I felt above me the moon's great eye.

There, alone, where a moment before
  Two were struggling, was only one!
"Thank God!" I cried, "he will love no more,
  And deceive no more—'tis done!"

The hate that had blazed so fierce calmed down
  Slowly, until of its raging glow
Only the ashes were left. The frown
  Cleared away from my knotted brow.
In the trough of my passion's swell I lay,
  And a sickening calm across me crept,
As the satiate passions slank away
  Drunk with revenge, and slept.

The deed was done! but an ugly fear
  Came over me now to touch this thing.
There was nothing to struggle against me here
  In this lifeless heap; I wished it would spring
And grasp me, and strike at me as it did
  Only a moment or two before.
I lifted the head, but it dropped and slid
  From my grasp to its bed of gore.

Coward! 'tis but a carcass that's dead!
  Lift it; drag it along the wood!
No one is looking—carefully spread
  Dry leaves over the stains of blood!
Hark!—ah! 'tis but the rustling leaves,
  As the freshening night-wind lifts and dies;
'Tis but the wind that sighs and grieves—
  No eye sees but the starry eyes!

What will you do with this horrible thing?
  Down! and grub a grave in the ground!
Grub with your nails! If you choose, you may sing
  That song of his. Don't start and look round!
'Tis but a corpse you are burying now—
  Surely that is a Christian deed—
How she would thank you!—clear your brow—
  What else do you ask or need?

Dig!—how terribly slow you are!
  The dawn in the east begins to grow;
The birds are all chirping—bury there
  That body at once, and for God's sake go!

The world will be up in less than an hour,
And rattle and ring along the road—
Dig for your life !—ah, well ! that's o'er !
And he lies in his last abode.

Speed o'er the country, slink to your room,
Happy at last that the deed is done !
Why do you look so ?—surely the gloom
That clouded so long your life has gone !
Why do you shrink from the open street ?
Why should you hide from the gaze of men ?
Go ! tell her your night's work when you meet,
And surely she'll kiss you and love you then.

UNDER THE ILEXES.

[*Dedicated to A. I. T.*]

DARK ilexes above, dry sward below,
O'er which the flickering sunglobes come and go;
Beyond, the swooping valley roughed by lines
Ruled by the plough between the rows of vines;
O'er yellow sunburnt slopes the olives grey
Casting their rounded shadows; far away
A stately parliament of poised stone-pines;
Dark cypresses with golden balls bestrewn,
Each rocking to the breeze its solemn cone;
Dim mountains, veiled in dreamy mystery,
Sleeping upon the pale and tender sky;
And near, with softened shades of purple brown,
By distance hushed, the peaceful mellowed town,

Domes, roofs, and towers all sleeping tranced and still—
A painted city on a painted hill.

Here let me lie and my siesta take,
And gaze about me, dreaming, half awake.

What peace is here! what rapt tranquillity!—
The far-off voices seem to lull the sense;
The cock's clear crow sounds faint and drowsily;
The sharp fly buzzing round the leafy fence;
The burning wasp, the bees that droning hum
Along the shining spires of withered grass;
The far cathedral bell's half-buried boom;
The leaves that whisper as the breezes come,
And talk a moment with them as they pass,
Break not the calm;—with half-shut dreaming eyes
I watch them, while my idle fancies stray,
Even as these noiseless yellow butterflies,
That poise on grass or flower, and drift away
Like wavering leaves in their perpetual play.
And all these sounds come vague to me and seem
Drowned in the air, like voices in a dream.

Look at this ilex-trunk's mosaic bark,
With all its myriad cracks, and seams, and squares !
See with what patient pains and happy cares
'Tis painted o'er with lichens light and dark,
Rich brown, pale grey, and softest malachite,
And every hue that can the eye delight !
This moss of golden green that round it clings,
Is a vast forest filled with noiseless things,
That 'neath its jungle make their secret lairs.
Here the black ant may hunt as in a park,
Here hosts of beetles come in burnished mail,
On secret errands bent from underground ;
Some with vermilion corselets on their back,
Marked with black crosses, some with gold em-
    browned,
Some bronzed with shadowy green, some ribbed and
    black,
Splendid as mortal knight was never found.
Here creeps the torpid locust from his cell,
Deep at its roots, to shed his silvery shell,
Breaks the thin crust, and spreads his gauzy wings,
And in the shade his praise of summer sings.

Here, in the centre of his woven wheel,
That dimly glistening in the shadow shakes,
Hangs the fat spider, ready and aware,
Round the fierce fly that pertinacious there
Darts to and fro, his silvery coil to reel.
Here the slim dragon-fly her visit makes
On glassy vans that gleam with opal hues,
And waves her tail of green enamelled rings.
Here the black grillo burrows all day long;
And peeping forth when fall the twilight dews,
Trills to the night its little simmering song.
Here creep among the grass, at work, or game,
Swarms of strange life that scarcely own a name;
Here live, and love, and fight, and sleep, and die,
Plagued by no dreams of immortality.
World within world, the deeper that we gaze,
Life widens, death recedes, the mass inert
Moves into being; all this mould and dirt
Is living in its own mysterious ways.

Which shall we dare most wonderful to call,
The infinite great, or not less infinite small?

Puzzled I gaze upon this spiring grass
That 'neath me lies, and ask,—can aught surpass
The wonder of this life minute that moves
Beneath my hand, and struggles, suffers, loves?
Are the vast worlds that darkness shows to night,
Or day enshrouds in its abyss of light,
More strange than this that hides from human eye
In the minuteness of its mystery?

No more! the shadows shrink; the prying sun
Hath found me out. The morning's gone—how soon!
The far cathedral bell is striking noon.
This sketch, dear Annie, is for you—half done.

OPHELIA.

THE rising wind o'er wold and hill
  Blows dreary, leadening all the lake;
  And all the whitened willows shake,
And twilight closes blear and chill.

The mist hangs thickening o'er the sea,
  A spectral light is in the sky,
  And all the branches creak and sigh,
And my heart sighs with them drearily.

Oh where is love that once was mine?
  Speak, oh my heart, and tell me where!
  Tell me, oh wind! whose wild despair
Is wrestling with the straining pine!

I rock its corpse so cold and pale,
  I braid its hair and kiss its eyes,
  And deck it with sweet memories;
Yet what can tears and moans avail?

Oh call it back to life again,
  With all its tones of youth and spring;
  Or break at once the throbbing string
That jars so wildly in my brain.

The past is past,—with sullen moan,
  Oh dreary wind, I hear you cry!
  And all the struggling trees reply,
Alone, alone, alone, alone.

THE RIVER OF TIME.

Oh! the river that runs for ever,
The rapid river of time!
The silent river, that pauses never,
Nor ceases its solemn rhyme!

How swift by the flowery banks it rushes,
Where love and joy are at play,
And stretch out their hands with laughter and blushes,
And beg it in vain to stay!

How slow through the sullen marsh of sorrow
It creeps with a lingering pain;
When night comes down and we long for the morrow,
And longing is all in vain!

O'er sparkling shoals of glittering folly,
 O'er deeps of dreadful crime,
O'er gladness and madness and melancholy,
 Through fears and hopes sublime,

Ruthlessly on in waking or sleeping,
 Unheeding our wish or will,
Through loving and laughing, and wailing and weeping,
 It bears us for good or ill—

Bears us down with a fearful motion,
 In a current no eye can see,
Down to the vast mysterious ocean
 We call eternity.

RENUNCIATION.

Oh no! you shall not catch me in the snare—
    I will not love, I say!
Life might become a terror, a despair,
    If you were ta'en away.

Nothing is given here, 'tis only lent,—
    I will not, dare not, trust:
For joy might strike at once his heaven-built tent,
    And leave me but its dust.

What horror, after all my life was given,
    Adventured in one bark,
If that should go, even to the joy of heaven,
    And I left in the dark!

Left on a wreck of sorrow, with no power
My losses to repair;
With death denied, and every torturing hour
By memory made a snare.

Left with the dregs of life, its wine poured out;
Left to the past a prey;
From its sad ghosts that haunt my heart about,
Helpless to flee away.

No! I renounce life's bliss—love's perfect flower,
Sweet though it be!—I choose
The lower, lasting lot, and keep the power,
Without a pang, to lose.

NIGHT-WATCH.

[*Dedicated to J. O. S.*]

NIGHT the mysterious, silent, solemn night,
    Broods over all!
Time, sweeping onward to the infinite,
    No sound lets fall.
We hear alone its heavy lifting breath
    Of deep repose,
As turning slowly in its dream of death
    The great earth goes.

Above, below, is silence! In the deep
    Of the vast sky,
In the low hollows where the white mists heap
    And shroud-like lie,

On the far plains where ghostlike in the shade
Dim olives dwell,
O'er slumbering city, forest, sea, is laid
Night's secret spell.

Tranced in the silence of this mystery,
An awe intense
Of all that is, and was, and is to be,
Weighs on the sense;
And shapeless thoughts and disembodied dreams
That end in sighs,
Sad memories, longings vague, and vanished schemes,
Before me rise.

Cease, ye wild thoughts! In duty's narrow bound
Alone is peace!
Oh infinite sea! that plummet cannot sound,
In thy abyss
Of wild conjecture we but sink and drown.
The awful breath
That blows from out the future bears us down
To fear,—to death.

A LEGEND.

HIGH noon in Acre blazed, and all the throng
Had sought the shade, when striding stern along
The burning street, and through the open square,
With feet unsandalled and dishevelled hair,
Was seen a figure strange, mysterious, tall,
With face uncovered, yet unknown to all.
Round her she gazed with wild impassioned look,
And in one hand a flaming torch she shook
High o'er her head, and in the other bore
A jar with water brimmed and running o'er,—
And with a high clear voice she cried, "Behold!
I will burn heaven up with this torch I hold,

And with this jar of water I, as well,
Will quench for ever all the fires of hell,
So that when heaven and hell alike are gone,
Man may love God, for God's own sake alone."

IN THE GARDEN.

Summer is dying, slowly dying—
  She fades with every passing day;
In the garden alleys she wanders, sighing,
  And pauses to grieve at the sad decay.

The flowers that came with the spring's first swallow,
  When March crept timidly over the hill,
And slept at noon in the sunny hollow—
  The snowdrop, the crocus, the daffodil,

The lily, white for an angel to carry,
  The violet, faint with its spirit-breath,
The passion-flower, and the fleeting, airy
  Anemone—all have been struck by death.

Z

Autumn the leaves is staining and strewing,
And spreading a veil o'er the landscape rare;
The glory and gladness of summer are going,
And a feeling of sadness is in the air.

The purple hibiscus is shrivelled and withered,
And languid lolls its furry tongue;
The burning pomegranates are ripe to be gathered;
The grilli their last farewell have sung;

The fading oleander is showing
Its last rose-clusters over the wall,
And the tubes of the trumpet-flower are strewing
The gravel-walks as they loosen and fall;

The crocketed spire of the hollyhock towers,
For the sighing breeze to rock and swing;
On its top is the last of its bell-like flowers,
For the wandering bee its knell to ring.

In their earthen vases the lemons yellow,
The sun-drunk grapes grow lucent and thin,

The pears on the sunny espalier mellow,
  And the fat figs swell in their purple skin;

The petals have dropped from the spicy carnation;
  And the heartless dahlia, formal and proud,
Like a worldly lady of lofty station,
  Loveless stares at the humble crowd.

And the sunflower, too, looks boldly around her;
  While the bella-donna, so wickedly fair,
Shorn of the purple flowers that crowned her,
  Is telling her Borgian beads in despair.

See! by the fountain that softly bubbles,
  Spilling its rain in the lichened vase,
Summer pauses!—her tender troubles
  Shadowing over her pensive face.

The lizard stops on its brim to listen,
  The butterfly wavers dreamily near,
And the dragon-flies in their green mail glisten,
  And watch her, as pausing she drops a tear—

Not as she stood in her August perfection !
  Not as she looked in the freshness of June !
But gazing around with a tender dejection,
  And a weary face like the morning moon.

The breeze through the leafy garden quivers,
  Dying away with a sigh and moan :
A shade o'er the darkening fountain shivers,
  And Summer, ghost-like, hath vanished and gone.

SYMBOLS.

[*Dedicated to E. M. S.*]

STILL hearts, whose passions never stir,
  At times I envy your repose!
Smooth lakes, where coyest wild-fowl whir,
  Ye feel no troublous ebbs and flows!

Yet, tropic hearts, your fiercer play
  Of sun and storm, of noon and night,
Is dearer than perpetual day
  In Arctic summer's glacial light.

Great clouds, which bear upon your backs
  The sunshine, in your breasts the storm—

Alps of the air, whose pathless tracks
  Ye course with ever-changing form;

By morning touched with aureole light;
  At sunset stranded—firing far
Your dull distress-guns—or at night
  Raced through by many a startled star—

Ye are the types that Genius loves!
  So, moulded by an inward stress,
A shade, a storm, it o'er us moves,
  A power to threaten or to bless.

IN THE SHADOW.

AND can it be that all is o'er—
  That I shall never see you more?
Or is it but a dream of night,
  That soon will pass with morning's light?
Oh! is the joy I used to own
  So lost, beyond the power to save;
And can it be that you are gone,
      And in the grave?

Not young, perhaps, as others see,
  Yet ever young you seemed to me;
The same sweet smile and tender art
  Remained, that first beguiled my heart;

The same dear look and gentle tone
  That ever its fresh welcome gave—
And can it be that you are gone,
    And in the grave?

Some silver lines were in your hair,
  But yet I never saw them there:
The years went on to you and me
  So gently and so evenly,
That scarce it seemed a week had flown
  Since first to me your love you gave—
And can it be that you are gone,
    And in the grave?

Something I miss at every turn—
  Something for which I blankly yearn;
And still some question to decide
  I turn as you were at my side—
I turn and think—ah! she alone
  Will give the counsel that I crave!
And then I feel that you are gone,
    And in the grave!

Henceforth, I know, at close of day,
When I return the old, old way,
The voice that greeted me before,
Soon as my hand was on the door,
No more will greet me with the tone
Of gentle welcome once it gave—
For oh! I feel that you are gone,
And in the grave.

Others such grief as mine have borne,
And I, like them, shall live and mourn,—
It nought avails to grieve or sigh
For what has gone so utterly!
And yet, how can I help to moan
For what no love had power to save—
For oh! I feel that you are gone,
And in the grave.

Courage! the heavy hand of Fate
Has laid on me its cruel weight,
And all these coming years of care
And sorrow I alone must bear;

Yes! I must strive to bear alone,
Without the help that once you gave;
For you, my love, my joy, are gone,
And in the grave.

ART.

[*Dedicated to G. H.*]

Is this the stately shape I saw
  In Greece a thousand years ago;
Who ruled the world by Beauty's law,
  And used among the gods to go?

Who, wheresoe'er she turned her eyes,
  Below her saw a reverent throng;
Whose praise was taken as a prize;
  Who made immortal with a song?

Now, scant in garb, a mendicant,
  She stretches forth her prayerful palms,

And wealth, in pity for her want,
  Contemptuous tosses her its alms.

This gift is not for charity,
  But love, that at thy feet I lay.
Oh, take my heart that throbs for thee!
  And smile as in the ancient day.

ON THE SEA-SHORE.

THE sky is grey, with lowering clouds of lead,
  And scarce a break of blue,
Here pencilled down with rain, and overhead
  With silver gleams shot through.

Upon the rocky shore I sit alone;
  The dark-green sullen sea,
Along the shore makes a perpetual moan,
  And struggles restlessly.

Noiseless as pictures, on their wings of white
  The distant vessels glide

By purple islands veiled in dreamy light,
That silent there abide.

Across the purple shoals of sunken rocks
The toppling racers break,
And suck, and roar, and beat with ceaseless shocks
The worn cliff's weedy base.

Heaved by the lifting swell, the long green flag
Of sea-weed floats and falls,
And down their shelf the raking pebbles drag,
As back the surf-wave crawls.

I sit as in a dream, and hear, and see,
With senses lulled away,
And what the ocean says or sings to me
I strive in vain to say.

Something there is beneath that constant moan
That utterance seeks in vain;
Like some dim memory, some hidden tone,
That, helpless, haunts the brain.

But all my thoughts, like sea-weed, swing and sway,
  The sport of fantasy;
And visions pass before me far away,
  Like vessels out at sea,—

Pass through my mind with an ideal freight,
  And softly move along—
A sweet procession, without care or weight,
  Like disembodied song.

THE CHIFFONIER.

I AM a poor Chiffonier!
I seek what others cast away!
In refuse-heaps the world throws by,
Despised of man, my trade I ply;
And oft I rake them o'er and o'er,
And fragments broken, stained, and torn,
I gather up, and make my store
Of things that dogs and beggars scorn.
I am the poor Chiffonier!

You see me in the dead of night
Peering along with pick and light,

And while the world in darkness sleeps,
Waking to rake its refuse-heaps;
I scare the dogs that round them prowl,
And light amid the rubbish throw,
For precious things are hid by foul
Where least we heed and least we know.
I am the poor Chiffonier!

No wretched and rejected pile,
No tainted mound of offal vile,
No drain or gutter I despise,
For there may lie the richest prize;
And oft amid the litter thrown,
A silver coin—a golden ring
Which holdeth still its precious stone,
Some happy chance to me may bring.
I am the poor Chiffonier!

These tattered rags, so soiled and frayed,
Were in a loom of wonder made,
And beautiful and free from shame
When from the master's hand they came.

The reckless world that threw them off
Now heeds them only to despise;
Yet, ah! despite its jeer and scoff,
What virtue still within them lies!
I am the poor Chiffonier!

Yes! all these shreds so spoiled and torn,
These ruined rags you pass in scorn,
This refuse by the highway tost,
I seek that they may not be lost;
And, cleansed from filth that on them lies,
And purified and purged from stain,
Renewed in beauty they shall rise
To wear a spotless form again.
I am the poor Chiffonier!

BLANK QUESTIONINGS.

WHAT is this vague, dim world before,
We vainly struggle to explore
With outstretched wishes, hopes, and thoughts,
That fail before they reach the shore?

What is this startling, sudden change,
That in a moment from the range
Of every sense takes life away
To regions dim and strange?

Dear friend! my earnest following thought
Thy track into that world hath sought

In vain; no word nor silent sign
  Of what, and where thou art, is brought.

  And yet I seem to feel that thou
  Beholdest me more nearly now,
And all my soul, like some clear book,
  Readest, I see not how.

  And knowing, now that life has fled,
  Thou, silent and unseen, may'st thread
The dim, still chambers of my soul—
  I feel, as with a holy dread,

  How full of love it ought to be,
  How pure of thought, how clean and free
From any stain and soil of sense,
  Which thy dear eyes could see.

  Come, then, when I am sad and low,
  And through those chambers softly blow
The fragrance of thy love around,
  And seeds of purer purpose sow.

Come! find the secret memories
That are not seen of human eyes—
The thoughts, the hopes, the dreams, that dwell
In inmost privacies.

And if thou findest, entering there,
Some nooks that are not wholly bare
Of love, forgive them for that love,
The evil and unfair.

ALPINE SONG.

WITH alpenstock and knapsack light
  I wander o'er hill and valley,
I climb the snow-peak's flashing height
  And sleep in the sheltered chalet,—
Free in heart—happy and free—
This is the summer life for me.

The city's dust I leave behind
  For the keen, sweet air of the mountain,
The grassy path by the wild rose lined,
  The gush of the living fountain,—
Free in heart—happy and free—
This is the summer life for me.

High above me snow-clouds rise
  In the early morning gleaming;
And the patterned valley beneath me lies
  Softly in sunshine dreaming,—
Free in heart—happy and free—
This is the summer life for me.

The bells of wandering herds I list
  Chiming in upland meadows;
How sweet they sound, as I lie at rest
  Under the dark pine shadows!—
Glad in heart—happy and free—
This is the summer life for me.

The thundering lawine's roar I hear,
  And the torrent's foamy bounding;
And the steep crag's answer sweet and clear,
  When the alpine horn is sounding,—
Glad in heart—happy and free,
This is the summer life for me.

A good stout alpenstock in hand,
  A flask from my shoulder swinging,
And a rose in my hat, o'er the Oberland
  I wander for ever singing,—
Glad in heart—happy and free,
This is the summer life for me.

TWO STARS.

Look! love, into the sky, and say,
When I am gone beyond the sea,
What stars of all the many stars
Shall shine for you and me.

See! there above, in Charles's Wain,
Those two, that close together shine,
One bright and large—*that* shall be yours—
The little faint one, mine.

The little one, that has no praise
From all who look—the satellite—
I know not if it have a name,
It shrinks so out of sight.

EUROPA.

A PICTURE BY PAUL VERONESE.

ZEPHYR is wandering here with gentle sound
The first fresh fragrance of the spring to seek ;
The milk-white steer, whose budding horns are crowned
With flowery garlands, kneeling on the ground
Receives his burden fair, and turns his sleek
Mild head around, her sandalled foot to lick ;
Luxuriant, joyous, fresh, with roses bound
About her sunny head, and on her cheek
The glow of morn, Europa mounts the steer.
One handmaid clasps her girdle, and one calls
The hovering loves to bring their garlands near.
From her full breast the loosened drapery falls,
As borne by Love o'er slope and lea she goes,
Glad with exuberant life—fresh as a new-blown rose.

GIOTTO'S CHAPEL,

PADUA.

How sweet the mild retirement of this spot!
This area, where the gladiator bled,
With turf and flowers is softly carpeted;
These girdling walls where later knighthood fought
Now draped with ivy stand, remembering not
Their scenes of former life. But here, instead,
The artist's steps in pilgrimage are led
To seek the shrine by Giotto's genius wrought.
Here, dedicate to art and piety,
His simple chapel stands; and painted here
Upon its walls a pictured life I see,
Inspired by feeling, earnest and sincere.
What faith, what simple dignity and grace
Art since hath lost, are in this cloistered place!

S C H E R Z I

BLUE BEARD'S CABINETS.

[*Dedicated to E. B. H.*]

WOMEN are curious, one and all, we know,—
Eve was, and so is every woman since.
All other virtues unto you are given
Except to close your eyes and curb your tongue.
Nor should I dare, dear Fatima, to you,
Best of your sex, to trust this single key,
Forbidding you to turn it in the lock ;—
You pout, say no ! and shake your pretty head—
Vainly—I know 'twould never let you rest.
Since mother Eve, a thing prohibited
Tortures your sex till it is known and tried.

Just try you? 'Tis a shame to say such words.
What have you ever done? When trust is gone,
Love follows soon—and are those really tears?
Tears? and we married only two short months—
Smile, dearest, once again, and take the key!

Take it! there's nothing better in the world
Than curiosity. It is the spur
Of knowledge. Pray, forgive me, Fatima!
Take it—I meant to leave you all the rest,
For these two months have slipped so swift away
(Joy flies so fast, 'tis only grief that halts)
In this our Spanish castle, that in truth
I had forgotten all the curious things
In the old cabinets;—but now, constrained
To leave you for a week, Annie and you
May hunt them through to while the hours away.

Here are the keys—each opes a cabinet
Where all of rare my ancestors have found,
Whether in travel through the broad domain
Of fact, or fancy, or romance, are ranged.

Each has its number. Enter! open all!
Stay! just to show how false is tongue of man,
Let me prohibit one! I will not say
What it contains. Thank you for that proud smile!
Think you I fear lest you should enter there;
No, by my love! You need not promise me.
I only say, This opes the door of death
Beyond the hall of dreams. You look surprised!
Curious, of course, you're not! There is the key!

These nine-and-ninety keys ope worlds enough
For one short week; and in the hall of death
Sooner or later all of us shall look.
Meanwhile, the others may suffice you. Stop!
Let me point out some curious cabinets
That will amuse you most, and mark the keys.

This, turned within its wards, will show you gems
Of wondrous beauty and strange rarity.
Red trees of branching coral, found beneath
The Elysian isles, and by the shining scales
Of mermaids polished, over-roof the hall;

And dragons, gleaming in enamelled mail,
With eyes of diamond, in the corners crouch.
In frieze of beaten gold, along the wall,
Struggle fierce centaurs clasped by Lapithæ.
And round the pavement whirls a chariot race,
With foaming steeds and naked outstretched arms
Mosaic'd on a band of marble black.
The ceiling's panels are in ivory carved,
Each with a lotus or magnolia spread,
And all the solid beams are massive gold.

Here, round the walls, in ebon cabinets
With ivory intarsia storied o'er,
And faced with flawless crystal, you may see
My stores of curious gems;—clear crystal balls,
Concealing in their depths a magic life,
Where steal the pale reflections of time's ghosts;
Cat eyes, whose iris circles glare and shift;
Opals, alive within with quivering fires;
Smooth globes of garnets like rich jelly-drops;
And mystic onyxes with figures strange
Carved on their facets by Egyptian priests;

Vases of jasper red and sardonyx,
Beryl and topaz, jacinth, amethyst,
And orient alabaster; and all stones
That sun-struck Africa, of dark and veined,
Blood-streaked and solemn, in her caves conceals;
The great carbuncle, sought for centuries,
Here blazes like a sun; and at its side
Note, too, a common stone, a pebble vile,
Hung near a pure and perfect chrysolite
(Smooth as a mirror, flawless as the sky);
It scarce would take your eye, it seems so vile,
Yet touched by it the filthiest dross grows gold,
And Europe for that stone would sell its soul.
Here is the pearl the Egyptian queen dissolved,
What time with Anthony in revels wild
She toyed and feasted; and beside it lies
The royal asp, her bracelet, where she kept
Her death, her freedom, in one poison-drop.
Pass not the Gracchi jewels, famed so long,
Two great cornelians, and beyond all price;
Nor the vast diamond Polyphemus wore
Fixed to his forehead, called by men his eye.

Here hangs a curtain ; draw it back—it runs
On rings that from the field of Cannæ came—
Behind it other curious rings you'll find—
Morone's, whence a prisoned devil spoke ;
Aboukir's, gifted with a lightning sword,
Which, when his hand waved, sheared his foeman's
  head ;
Joudar's, which owned its black tremendous slave ;
The Samian's lucky ring he could not lose ;
And Pyrrhus's, whose figures nature carved ;
And that which Gyges wore ; and Solomon's,
Whose mystic stamp sealed in his sunken vase
The cloud-vast Afrite 'neath the Arabian lake ;
There is the ring with which my ancestor
Married the Adriatic—one sea-green
Aqua marina, jutting forth in points
Of starry brilliants ; and beside it lies
The poison-ring the gold-haired Borgia wore ;
And that Elizabeth to Essex gave.

This iron key, with lines of silver veined,
Opens a cabinet more curious yet.

Ultramarine the roof, one mighty block,
Besprinkled with a thousand golden stars.
Panelled in Afric marbles are the walls,
All pictured o'er with wild and mystic shapes
Of every varying hue,—from purpling lakes
And crimson carmines unto Stygian black.
Two sombre columns carved with stories strange
Of Asian magic in the centre stand—
The capital's red gold a band of skulls.
As the vast door you push, a thunderous sound
Of mournful music groans along the vault,
And lightnings, flashing, cross their jagged swords.
Be undismayed and enter! On the floor
A charm is written; in the circle stand
And say "Geheimniss!" Music then will rain
Soft as a summer shower to soothe the sense,
And hands invisible will lead you round.

Here you will find the wondrous planisphere
Of Abdelsamad, in whose depths were seen
All regions of the earth—that smote with fire
The nations at its owner's wrathful nod.

Here I have ranged a thousand curious things
Found in my travels into distant lands ;—
Among them is a hydra's snaky head ;—
And (for I'm curious in hair) you'll find,
Bound in a single braid, and closely clasped
By a dried Harpy-claw, one Gorgon lock
From the Medusa's head, entwined with one
Torn from Megæra and Tisiphone,
And from Alecto one—while in and out
A golden tress that on the Borgia's brow
Meandered once, slips gleaming here and there.

Here are some relics which from over sea
The Flying Dutchman brought from classic lands.
Among them is Pandora's opened box,
The Attic cynic's lantern and his tub,
A shrieking branch from the Æneid grove,
Arion's harp and Hermes' wand ; the bag
Of Eolus, Ulysses' wax, the flute
That Orpheus played ; a soft half-melted plume
Dropped from the waxen wings of Icarus,
The sword suspended by a single hair. . . .

And underneath this last a skull I've placed—
One that was brought to me from Golgotha.

Here from the vaguer regions of Romance
Are various objects, and beyond all price :
Such as the cap which Fortunatus wore,
The bowl in which the men of Gotham sailed,
The bodkin that Amina used to pick
Her grains of rice before her fouler feast,—
Agrippa's glass and that of Schemseddin,
The King of Thule's goblet, with a tinge
Of the red wine that wet his noble beard,
Poor Schlemihl's shadow, and the Roc's huge egg,
Aladdin's lamp, and Circe's magic cup.

Here in one corner of the room you'll find
A medley of all sorts of oddities :
There's a wise saw, that shows its teeth to fools,
An ancient augur (famous as a bore),
A modern screw, a rod in pickle kept,
A pair of ruined breaches made by Time,
And in them tares the enemy hath sown.

Here is the crystal luck of Eden hall,
In which some flowers of rhetoric are placed—
The snowy plume of Henry of Navarre,
With Conachar's white feather at its side—
Here is a tune that from Munchausen's horn
Was taken ere it thawed, and fragments rare
Of frozen music sent me by De Staël,—
Being choice bits of fluting round the drum
Of Kubla Khan's majestic pleasure dome—
You'll know the spot by looking on the floor,
Where I have caused a pattern to be worked
In coloured jewels, after a design
From the Mosaic dispensation drawn—
While from the ceiling o'er it like a lamp
Hangs the lost Pleiad, which the wandering Jew
Found on the topmost peak of Ararat.

This my menagerie will ope, and here
Along the walls are pictured various lands:
While columns with alternate ebon bands
Winding with ivory spirals stand between—
Here Asian deserts, idly vast, outstretch,

And black Nigritia scowls, and naked girls
Dance in the shade of Abyssinian palms—
Here shakes the tinkling life of the Chinese
'Neath Altai mountains in Mongolia;
While on the other side the slim canoe
Through Polynesian waters swiftly glides;
And the great banyan darkens down the shore.

Along the northern wall the iceberg sails,
Toppling and crashing through white fields of ice,
Where the bear souses in his Arctic bath.
Close by, beneath the Uralian avalanche,
Siberia spreads her dark platoons of pines.
All lands are here—all quarters of the earth—
Venetian splendours of her gorgeous days—
The savage life afar in western wilds—
The babbling glitter of the Boulevards—
The lonely Kaffir's hut—the middle sea,
With roaring billows plunging all alone.

Here range my wondrous animals, and here
The great white elephant of Siam walks

Beside the magic steed that swam the air,
And Pegasus with both his wings tied down.
Here is Androcles' lion; at his side
Chimæra and three-headed Cerberus;
And near the dragon with a hundred heads,
That watched the Hesperian gardens day and night,
Couches the sad Sphinx with her silent face.
Strange converse hold they in a wondrous tongue,
And many a tale of ancient days they tell,
Of Orpheus, Hercules, Bellerophon,
Growling a laugh the while from ruddy maws.
Rouse them from sleep! for now with habits changed
And wearied with the sleepless hours of eld
They slumber much.

But not to pause with these,
Look at my Attic hive. Hymettus' flowers
Are blooming round it. There is Rhaicus' bee,
And one that Sappho caught on Cupid's lips,
Which stung her to a luscious epigram.
Here in sheep's clothing wanders Æsop's wolf,
With Reineke the diplomatic fox,

And Monsieur Frog who burst with vanity.
Here too 's the cow that vaulted o'er the moon,
The famous clock the mouse ran up, the cat
That owned the fiddle, the small dog that laughed
When crafty dish with silly spoon eloped,
And mother Hubbard's still more famous dog.
Here is the goose that laid the golden egg,
The camel through the needle's eye that passed,
Quarles' friendly monkey, Beauty's gentle beast,
The tortoise with the hare that ran a race,
And that which crushed the skull of Æschylus.
Here in a pleasant group you may behold
The Austrian eagle with its double head,
The Scottish unicorn and Gallic cock,
Discussing politics and talking wise
Of European balances of power.
And here in pleasant conversation meet
Two long-eared friends, who hold a wise discourse
With longer-horned companions scarce so dull
As many a human party we have known.
There Balaam's social beast, and at his side
His crony, Apuleius' golden ass,

May yet be seen talking with Myron's cow,
Or the red cow that told such wondrous tales
Of her interior knowledge of Tom Thumb;
While standing near and listening, you may see
A group of bulls—among them he who pulled
Cock Robin's knell, and he whom Phaleris
Begat in brass, and one from Ireland sent,
And from the Vatican one Papal bull.
And here at last, to end my catalogue,
Which merely hints a creature here and there,
My rarest wonders from the East, you'll see
Two vampires and a red-lipped female Ghoule.

Tired of these, if you should wish to read,
Look in my library. This curious key—
A serpent issuing from an ivory skull
And twisting round its handle—opens it.
Here are dim alcoves framed in ebony
And lit by softly-blazoned diamond panes,
Where glow and move as if endowed with life
The painted history of glorious men.
Each pane is magic; at a simple sign

The life of him whose name is writ beneath
Will glide in mute procession o'er its face.
The room is deaf to sound ; a moth-like veil
Like woven twilight o'er the ceiling floats,
And from the centre hangs a crystal globe:
Touch it but once, a Marid answers it,
And at your nod brings all your wish may shape.
Noiseless he moves, and comes and goes like air,
Waving Arabian odour from his wings.
Would you behold the furthest wildest spot
Hid in the secret'st corner of the earth,
Twirl the globe thrice and in its depths it lives.
Fixed in the wall a magic mirror shines
Oblong and veined with myriad wavering lines :
That's the time-table of the centuries—
Name but the number of a year, day, hour,
And then a place—the deed there done, and then,
Will start at once to picture in the glass
And move, as you request it, on in time.

Within these cabinets are curious books,
Among a myriad which I will not name,

Which now the world supposes to be lost—
The Sibyl's books are there, the two she burnt,
There Dante's rhyme, with Angelo's designs,
There Raffaelle's hundred sonnets fairly writ,
There Sappho's songs, complete, and Shakespeare's life,
And the lost tragedies of Æschylus.
The famous distich of Callicrates
Writ on a seed of sesamum is there,
With the whole Iliad in a nutshell closed.
There is the music of the Song of songs,
Great books of drawings by Philostrates,
And all the poems Coleridge meant to write.
In the far corner towering over all
Chryselephantine sits the Phidian Zeus,
And on the walls Da Vinci's great cartoon
Beside its rival hangs intact and fresh;
And there alone upon a sombre stand,
Tempting the touch to open its great leaves,
Where no one ever read but wept, is placed
The sad black-letter Book of Destiny.

This key my great conservatory opes,

Where you will find some rare and curious fruits—
There are the sour grapes—but within your reach—
Taste them if you desire! There too you'll see
The apple Paris to the fairest gave;
And that which tempted Eve, in it her teeth
You'll see imprinted; also that which grows
Upon the Dead Sea's margin, with the three
That from the Hesperian gardens Atlas stole.
There is the date-stone by the merchant thrown
Against the Afrite o'er the garden-wall;
The pear that caused the sleeper's nose to grow;
The Lotus fruit that brings oblivion;
A date-tree with the dates of everything;
And the unripening fruit of our desires.

This opes the silent cabinet of dreams—
'Tis vague and empty when you enter first!
A mystery floats around, like music dim
For which the ear keeps straining—sounds so fine
That all the soul must listen, leaning out
Upon the furthest verge of sense to hear.
Out of the dark emerge, by slow degrees,

Vague things that come and go—great ghostly shapes—
Like shadows on a curtain when it swings;
Dear smiles gleam there that made the joy of life,
And hopes burst forth to their consummate flower
That faded long ago to death and dust
In our young hearts. Ambition there holds up
Its splendid gifts, and in our hands we grasp
The prize we covet dearer than our life.
There, lips are kissed that drown the soul with love,
And voices whisper us to heavenly trance,
And wishes reach their goal. There you may find
The cabala on which is fairly writ
The squaring of the circle—the receipt
For alchemists to make the wondrous stone,
And to achieve perpetual motion. There
Are faultless pictures, statues, poems, songs,
That sternest critics strive in vain to blame.
One cabinet contains, placed side by side,
A pair of shabby, little, worn-out shoes,
A golden locket with an auburn curl,
A dry dead rose, the yellow page whereon
The drawing of a childish hand is seen,

And a love-letter stained with blots of tears—
Ah ! touch them not, for they will make you weep !
There is a box crammed full of broken hopes
And childish joys we careless threw away
And never could recover, though lifelong
We prayed the truants to return again.

Here for a time, while sleep's dim door is shut,
What waking life denies, in dreams is given.
Here, sleeping, you may quaff the drink of gods,
And in a moment know perennial youth.
Nor this alone—but through the wilds of space,
Borne to the universe's verge, may rush
Up to the gates of heaven, and see below
In endless swarming all the fiery spheres
Flash through the solemn depths of silent night.

Pass through this room—'tis but a vestibule
That opens to a vaster drearier hall—
Where horrent dreams steal noiselessly about,
And opiate shapes of sick delirium swarm,
And nightmares wander. There the Marids dwell

And Ghouls, and Ginns, and Afrites huge and black,
And forms so faint that they elude the eye.
These, as you look upon them, shift and change,
Mow, mock, and threaten, and pursue your steps
As, wild with fear, you strive with leaden feet
To flee their presence. There, in awe and dread,
Vague horrors creep that have no name on earth,
Found in the fevered dreams of wicked souls,
And sent me from the East. There upward stretch,
Leading to nowhere, monstrous galleries,
Where slipping, sliding, goes the 'wildered thought
Up endless convolutions into heights
So vast we totter in a vague dismay
Or drop to blankness. There huge caverns gape,
Dripping with terrors, into which we slip
Despite our death-like graspings for support.
There whirl a million dizzy wheels of thought,
And spin to madness. With your waking steps
You need not fear them—they're unreal all.

Here stay your feet; nor curious seek to pass
The massive door that opens out beyond.

What lies behind, your eyes must never see—
Never without the charm to keep you safe,
For there lies death, unless the charm you own.
"Give it to me," you cry—so curious, then?
If you insist, of course; and you'll admit
Eve is your mother. Never say again
That women have no curiosity.
Ah! now you frown, and with a look of pride
Reject my offer. So, love, let it be.
I'll keep the charm, and say 'tis just as sure
That you are curious as that I'm unkind.
Both false—and here's the key, dear Fatima;
And pray obey my warning—never look
Into the Cabinet of Death, for there
A step were fatal if without the charm.
So fare you well.—Ah! I forgot to say
The key's a fairy that will tell me all.
Don't shake your finger at me, and curl up
That pretty lip with scorn. Better a kiss!
Perhaps I'd better leave the charm—no! no!
Not one word more—only a kiss—farewell!

SINGING AT TWILIGHT.

YOU sang the olden songs, and, sadly dreaming,
I lay and listened, while you thought I slept;
And if the tears were from my eyelids streaming,
You saw them not, and so I freely wept.

Round us the silent, shadowy night was stealing;
You were a voice alone within the dark;
And from life's hardened crust a tender feeling
Broke, like a blossom, through the rugged bark.

You were again a young and blushing maiden,
Who leaned upon my breast and breathed your love,

And I, no more with disappointments laden,
  Seemed, as of yore, beside you in the grove.

The sky above us was serenely tender,
  The moon shone softly gleaming through the trees;
Clasped heart to heart in Love's complete surrender,
  Life seemed an island in enchanted seas.

Dim longings, vague desires, like breaths from heaven,
  Thrilled all our being with a strange unrest;
And all the finest strings that God hath given
  Trembled to voiceless music in the breast.

Your hand's electric fire again ran through me,
  I breathed the hyacinth odour of your hair;
Your soul in long sweet kisses clung unto me,
  And filled me with a rapturous despair.

Your voice had ceased; yet still around me fluttered
  The visions that your songs had raised in me;
When—" Mr Jones," cried Jeames—" Curse Jones," I muttered,
  And you—" Bring in the lights; 'tis time for tea."

I was again an old hard-hearted sinner,
 And you were fifty, and you wore a cap;
Laughing, you said to Jones, "After his dinner
 You see the old man likes to take his nap."

PERSICA.

OH Persica, Persica, pale and fair,
  With a ripe blush on your cheek,
How pretty—how very pretty you are,
  Until you begin to speak!

As for a heart and soul, my dear,
  You have not enough to sin;
Outside so fair, like a peach you are,
  With a stone for a heart within.

A MUSICAL BOX.

I KNOW her, the thing of laces, and silk,
  And ribbons, and gauzes, and crinoline,
With her neck and shoulders as white as milk,
  And her doll-like face and conscious mien.
A lay-figure fashioned to fit a dress,
  All stuffed within with straw and bran;
Is that a woman to love, to caress?
  Is that a creature to charm a man?

Only listen! how charmingly she talks
  Of your dress and hers—of the Paris mode—
Of the coming ball—of the opera-box—
  Of jupons, and flounces, and fashions abroad.

Not a bonnet in church but she knows it well,
  And Fashion she worships with downcast eyes;
A *marchande de modes* is her oracle,
  And Paris her earthly paradise.

She's perfect to whirl with in a waltz;
  And her shoulders show well on a soft divan,
As she lounges at night and spreads her silks,
  And plays with her bracelets and flirts her fan;
With a little laugh at whatever you say,
  And rounding her "No" with a look of surprise,
And lisping her "Yes," with an air *distrait*,
  And a pair of aimless, wandering eyes.

Her duty this Christian never omits!
  She makes her calls, and she leaves her cards,
And enchants a circle of half-fledged wits,
  And slim *attachés* and six-foot Guards.
Her talk is of people, who're nasty or nice,
  And she likes little bon-bons of compliments;
While she seasons their sweetness by way of spice,
  By some witless scandal she often invents.

Is this the thing for a mother or wife?
  Could love ever grow on such barren rocks?
Is this a companion to take for a wife?
  One might as well marry a musical box.
You exhaust in a day her full extent;
  'Tis the same little tinkle of tunes always;
You must wind her up with a compliment,
  To be bored with the only airs she plays.

ROSA HESTERNA.

Yes, my love, it was fresh and glowing,
  Blooming and beautiful,—yesterday!
Now its odour is sickly, its petals are going,
  Its beauty is vanished—throw it away!
Pray, don't thrust it under my nose!
Who can endure a yesterday's rose?

I cannot deny your pretty sayings—
  "It gave its life, and died in your hand,"
And "There are no deaths without decayings;"—
  But the dying of roses who can stand?
The sweeter the odour the worse the decay;
And a yesterday's rose!—oh, throw it away!

Gratitude,—pity,—sense of duty?
  Oh, my dear, don't talk such prose!
If duty don't rhyme, as you say, to beauty,
  Does yesterday's odour haunt yesterday's rose?
To-morrow, perhaps, I shall throw you away!
Perhaps, to-morrow, but not to-day.

Now, while your lips are fresh as roses,
  Kiss me, for preaching becomes you not!
Time for his wisdom his penance imposes;
  When things are ripe they begin to rot.
And our loves and our roses, when they decay,
However we sigh, must be thrown away.

SNOWDROP.

WHEN, full of warm and eager love,
  I clasp you in my fond embrace,
You gently push me back and say,
  "Take care, my dear, you'll spoil my lace."

You kiss me just as you would kiss
  Some woman friend you chanced to see ;
You call me "dearest."—All love's forms
  Are yours, not its reality.

Oh Annie ! cry, and storm, and rave !
  Do anything with passion in it !
Hate me an hour, and then turn round
  And love me truly, just one minute.

PRINTED BY WILLIAM BLACKWOOD AND SONS, EDINBURGH.

www.ingramcontent.com/pod-product-compliance
Lightning Source LLC
LaVergne TN
LVHW011151110826
845150LV00006B/1213

* 9 7 8 1 4 2 5 5 4 5 9 6 3 *